Sola Fide

by

FAITH

alone

Carol Round

**Passionate
Purpose
Publishing**

Sola Fide
by FAITH alone

Copyright © 2012 by Carol Round

Printed in the United States of America

Passionate Purpose Publishing

ISBN-13:
978-1479252275

CONTENTS

DEDICATION

To my precious grandchildren—
Cheyenne, Brennan, Cash,
Leah and Luke

"My prayer for each of you is that you will come to know Jesus,
not only as your Savior but as your best friend."

Acknowledgements

Since November 2005, I have sat down each week at my computer to write a newspaper column. Without the support, feedback and encouragement from my wonderful friends and church family, I would not have been able to weave 500-515 words each week into what has become a labor of love for me—*A Matter of Faith*. In this third collection of my columns, I would like to thank those individuals who always provide what I need at just the right time. Even encouragers need encouragement.

In no particular order, I would like to acknowledge:

Charlie Shotsky—who faithfully proofreads every column before it is sent for publication each week. Words are never enough to express my gratitude.

Clarice Doyle—whose friendship and faith are a balm to my weary soul when I want to give up.

Pastor Ray Crawford—whose faith, friendship and inspiration have helped me to grow spiritually.

Dorothy Willman Cummins—whose friendship is based on love and honesty. You always tell me the truth—even if it's not what I want to hear.

Mary Lou Peterson—whose determination to recover from a stroke has inspired me to keep putting one foot in front of the other.

Nathan Faught—whose insight and faith helped me to choose the right image for the cover of *Sola Fide*.

My faithful readers—whose feedback affirms that I am doing what God has called me to do.

Preface

Although I grew up attending church faithfully, and was baptized at age 14, I didn't realize Jesus wanted a personal relationship with me until a sunny October afternoon in 2001. I wandered to a nearby lake that afternoon in search of something to fill the emptiness left after my 28-year marriage ended. If you had asked me who I was, I don't know if I could have answered. I could have told you my name but my identity was lost. For the first time in my 47 years, I prayed aloud: "God, I need some direction in my life. Please help me."

Since that afternoon more than 10 years ago, my life with Jesus has been an adventure through heartache and laughter, pain and healing, surprises and disappointments, failure and growth, learning and loss. However, my Jesus has walked beside me and even carried me through difficult times, including the loss of both my parents, five surgeries in seven years—two for breast cancer, retirement from a 30-year teaching career and relocation within two months to a new community. These, along with other major life-changing events, have taught me to place my faith in the One who has numbered every hair on my head and who knows my words before I speak them.

Sola Fide, the Latin term for "by faith alone," is the doctrine that asserts God's pardon for guilty sinners, granted to and received through faith, conceived as excluding all "works," alone. We can't earn God's grace. It is a gift. We just have to accept it.

Since accepting His gift, I have learned to walk by faith, not by sight. For what is faith but the confident assurance that what we hope for is going to happen and the evidence of things we cannot yet see (Hebrews 11:1).

When I said, "Yes" to Jesus, I never dreamed I would be using my love of words to inspire others with His Word. Since November 2005, I have been writing a weekly faith-based column that currently runs in 12 Oklahoma newspapers and 2 online Christian publications with an international reach. Each week, before I write my column, I invite the Holy Spirit in and ask God to give me the words to reach the people He wants me to reach in the ways He knows best. Through His guidance, I have not missed a week since that time.

Living in God's Economy

"When they had all had enough to eat, he said to his disciples, "Gather the pieces that are left over. Let nothing be wasted"—*John 6:12(NIV).*

Growing up, I can recall my mother's admonition to eat everything on our plates. Of course, she used the old standby, "There are starving children in Africa." While my mother had good intentions, I didn't grasp the fact that there are people in our country and across the world who do not share in the abundance that most of us in this country do—and we are spoiled.

My sister and I were recently discussing the luxury of eating at a fast-food place when we were children. Although there were not many from which to choose, we still didn't eat out much. Our mother was a wonderful cook and good at using leftovers creatively. Nothing was wasted.

I am guilty, just like most of us in today's society, of wastefulness. As our society has become more affluent, so has our propensity to toss away, without a second thought, the leftovers. However, I'm not just talking about food.

Within months of purchasing a new techie gadget, another one is taunting us with the latest and greatest upgraded features that we think we need to keep up with a society constantly wired for sight and sound. Most, but not all, of our outdated gizmos end up in a drawer or in a landfill.

With the worldwide economic downturn, many have been forced to re-evaluate their priorities and revisit their values. Even though we understand the definition of economy in man's dictionary, in the context of the things of God we often don't comprehend.

According to a website, based on the ministries of Watchman Nee and Witness Lee who labored together to build up the local churches in China in the 1930s and 1940s, "God is like an immensely wealthy householder. He desires to dispense His unsearchable riches (Ephesians 3:8) to all of His people, but to accomplish this immense task He needs a plan, an arrangement, an economy."

While humans worry about their bank accounts and their 401(k), God's economy is even more valuable and comes with a guaranteed life assurance policy. It is based on carrying out His eternal purpose to satisfy His heart's desire. Ephesians 1:5 says, "He predestined us to be adopted as His sons through Jesus Christ, in accordance with his pleasure and will."

God longs to have a relationship with each of us. He was willing to pay a tremendous price through the death of His Son to fulfill His plan. In God's economy, Jesus Christ is everything.

In John 6, Jesus gives thanks for the five small barley loaves and two small fish that feed the 5,000. There was plenty to satisfy the physical hunger of everyone present with leftovers to spare. Jesus said, "Let nothing be wasted."

When we operate in God's economy, we want for nothing. Remembering that He is the Bread of Life should remind us that we should not waste our time or money on things that do not matter.

What matters most to you?

Two is Greater than One

> "But the man who looks intently into the perfect law that gives freedom, and continues to do this, not forgetting what he has heard, but doing it—he will be blessed in what he does"
> —*James 1:25 (NIV)*.

Unless I am looking in the mirror or putting on earrings, I forget sometimes that I have two ears. I also forget the mathematical equation that $2>1$.

Since I came out of the womb talking, I have to remind myself constantly to speak less and listen more. As I have grown in my Christian walk, I now understand why God gave us two ears and one mouth. He wants us to listen twice as much as we speak.

It is so tempting to let our tongue run loose when we think we have all the answers. However, God has a better plan, which includes our spiritual growth.

Although I don't watch much television, a recent morning news program captured my attention as I was putting on my make-up. The commentator was discussing how easy it is to find self-proclaimed experts who can "talk the talk" on TV. However, finding people who actually know what they're talking about is often a little more difficult, according to the newsperson.

If you listen to television or radio at all, you know you can't escape the ranting and raving of people spouting their opinions. As the newsperson said, "Pundits are everywhere, and they're almost always at full boil."

When I hear two or more people arguing over an issue, interrupting before the other has finished, I switch channels or hit the off button. And it's not just the rudeness that bothers me. Some of the time, the hatred that spews forth makes me wonder about the character of the people involved.

I did find this particular morning program interesting because the young man being interviewed aspires to pundit stardom. His take on the subject of experts follows: "I think that the better pundits are people who either can pretend they know a lot about something, so they're an expert at pretending, or they're an expert in the actual issue."

The word pundit, meaning "learned man or scholar," comes from the 17th century Sanskrit. However, the concept of shaping public opinion has been around for a much longer time.

If you think about it, Jesus shaped public opinion. He didn't, however, have to shout or disagree to get the audience's attention. His teachings about how the world should be inspired the chosen 12 to follow Him, eventually leading to the founding of the Christian faith.

My own faith has grown as I have learned to listen more and speak less. However, I have to remind myself frequently that without God's generosity in giving wisdom and not finding fault, I would not be where I am on my journey—and I haven't arrived yet.

God has called us to become mature and complete in our faith. This is a high calling.

Are you willing to listen and follow?

Shedding Your Stuff

"Dear children, keep yourselves from idols" –1 John 5:21 (NIV).

The headline grabbed my attention: "Americans shedding stuff for simpler life"

Because of shrinking paychecks, job losses and housing foreclosures, Americans are being forced to pare their lifestyles. Another concern, according to this article, involves the environment and the impact our wasteful lifestyle has had on the landscape.

Michael Maniates, a professor of political and environmental science at Allegheny College in Meadville, PA, had this to say about the current economic crisis, "Perhaps the silver lining is that people are coming to realize they can live with less and their lives are richer for it."

A 2009 MetLife Study of the American Dream reported that 47 percent of the consumers surveyed say they already have what they need, up from 34 percent in a November 2006 poll. In "Shed Your Stuff, Change Your Life," author Julie Morgenstern says, "People are feeling forced and inspired to get back to what is core to them. They are valuing objects less and experiences and people more."

After reading Morgenstern's book, Dan Bruno of San Diego, launched a "100 Thing Challenge" last November, saying he wanted to pare his own possessions to fewer than that. Eric Dykstra, a pastor in Minnesota read the book and Bruno's blog and began encouraging his congregation to trim their personal possessions to 100 items.

According to Dykstra, "People have really taken this to heart. They donated so much to charity, including boats, furniture and snow blowers, that they filled a warehouse.

"The purpose was to break the hold of materialism," he added. Dykstra pared his wardrobe from five suits to one, from a dozen ties to two. "It was very freeing."

Recently, my morning devotional was titled, "Unburdened?" Using Luke 18 for the scripture reference, the writer pointed out that when we consider the words of Jesus in this passage, we often think it is an indictment of the rich and a call to sell all possessions. However, if we only reflect on this view, we miss an important message for ourselves.

Jesus' message in this passage centers on the man searching for something to fill the emptiness that possessions cannot. The man sought Jesus because he wanted a closer relationship with God. However, he was unwilling to place his belief and trust in Jesus, who could fulfill that desire. He wouldn't sell his possessions.

Whatever our financial status, if we don't put God first, believing that He can and will meet our needs, we miss out on a life of meaning and purpose. I think people forget in our "marketing-crazed world" that the simple is what makes life worthwhile. I am reminded of this when I spend time with my grandchildren blowing inexpensive bubbles and running through the sprinkler. I tell them that we are making memories. No complicated battery-operated toy can replace that.

This quote from Maude Royden, English preacher and social worker, says it all, "When you have nothing left but God, then for the first time you become aware that God is enough."

Is God enough for you?

What's Joy Got to do with it?

"The Lord is my strength and my shield; my heart trusts in him, and I am helped. My heart leaps for joy and I will give thanks to him in song"— *Psalm 28:7 (NIV)*.

I start most days in good spirits when I remember who is in control of the universe. However, when I let the little irritations in life steal my joy, I have to refocus, regroup and re-find my way back to the One who provides my joy.

What's joy got to do with it? Everything. Sometimes, even as Christians, we fail to experience real joy, a fruit of the Holy Spirit, by letting three common "joy stealers" ruin our day: worry, stress and fear.

In his book *Laugh Again*, Charles Swindoll defines worry as "an inordinate anxiety about something that may or may not occur." And most of the time, what we worry about, never happens.

I've fought this joy stealer more times than I care to count. What if I don't have enough money to pay my monthly bills? I always do. What if my vehicle breaks down? It's never as bad as I think. What if…what if…what if?

What about stress, which is, according to Swindoll, "an intense strain over a situation we can't change or control?" How many of us have tried to change others, and their attitudes, and forgotten to take a long hard look at our own?

"Fear," according to Swindoll, "is a dreadful uneasiness over danger, evil or pain." Fear of the unknown, including the future, only magnifies our problems. It's like looking at an ant through a magnifying glass and seeing a space creature.

Christian author Ruth Senter said, "Joy is elusive. It flows most freely when we stop trying to make it happen. We do not come to joy. Joy comes to us."

Then, why do we fail to see the joy in everyday experiences that remind us God is in the small stuff as well as those times that threaten to choke the life out of us. I remember this when I spend time with my grandchildren.

Whether it is the sage advice of my five-year-old granddaughter or the impish grin of my four-year-old grandson, I find joy knowing that most of what I worry about, stress out over and fear, never happens. Their childlike faith is a reminder to me that happiness depends on happenings, but joy depends on Jesus.

While life is full of difficulties, we cannot let any situation rob us of our joy. A recent newspaper article about two children battling cancer grabbed my attention. In the midst of uncertainty, the families had bonded because the fathers discovered they were perfect blood type matches for each other's child. One father said, "If we hadn't been diagnosed with cancer, we wouldn't know the Howies. Our kids will be linked together for a long time."

When we remember that our joy is linked to our faith in the Lord then we can experience it even in the direst of circumstances.

Is your heart leaping for joy today?

Wanna Compare Notes?

"And our hope for you is firm, because we know that just as you share in our sufferings, so also you share in our comfort"
—2 Corinthians 1:7 (NIV).

In high school and college, I was blessed to be a good note taker. Those who were challenged to get good notes usually wanted to copy my detailed ones. This was especially critical in those classes where the teacher's lectures were the basis for all tests.

I not only took good notes but I would recopy them or type them for studying because it helped me to learn the materials. This was before the days of Microsoft, laptops and computer geeks, and I used a manual typewriter. I was born in 1953 so you do the math.

Math, however, was never my forte` so I had to rely on others to help me make it through my required classes. Thankfully, in those days, I only had to take three math classes before graduating with my high school diploma and only one semester of algebra to meet my college requirements. If it had not been for math whizzes who took pity on me, I probably wouldn't have made it.

I also wouldn't have made it this far in Life 101 without the prayers, advice, and support of my friends, especially those who know from where their hope comes. All of us have life stories that include hard times and moments when we've felt alone. No one is exempt from failures, mistakes and choices that have led us astray, causing heartache and regrets.

Recently, a pastor friend said, "We are all broken in some way." Sometimes our brokenness is obvious, leaving deep scars. Others, however, hide their hurts behind beautiful exteriors.

I think God places the right people in our paths at just the right moment. Seven years ago, I moved to a new community where I could count on one hand the number of people I knew. Since then, my network of support has grown. If I included all of my fingers and toes, it would still not be enough to calculate the blessings of those friendships.

Blessings multiply when you share them with others and troubles are divided when two or more share the load by listening, advising and praying with you. If one falls down, another can help you up.

Life can be overwhelming sometimes but when we compare notes by sharing our trials, we can find encouragement and hope. The same goes for sharing those times when God has transformed us. Perhaps, through our sharing, someone else's life will be changed. Or maybe, in your sharing, you will find your load lighter.

When we realize that our purpose for being is to help others, we can move forward in faith. Sometimes it is with baby steps; other times, God requires us to take giant leaps, not knowing what the future holds, but trusting Him to provide what we need along the way.

When we compare notes with others, we are reminded that God is always faithful.

Who needs your notes?

What's Your Word?

"Your word is a lamp for my feet, a light on my path"
—Psalm 119:105 (NIV).

"Guideposts" is my favorite magazine. This monthly inspirational magazine, designed to help readers achieve their maximum personal and spiritual potential, contains stories written by people from all walks of life. In the January 2012 issue, author Debbie Macomber shared her New Year's tradition and one I have since adopted.

At the beginning of each year, she reflects on the words that have appeared repeatedly in her life. By writing in her journal, she watches for patterns to develop. For example, in 1979, "hunger" was her word. Although she wasn't sure why she chose that word, she came to realize that, in part, it had to do with her lifelong struggle with her weight.

However, as that year unfolded, she realized that her physical hunger for food wasn't the only struggle she faced. She says, "There were other hungers as well. With four children in a tiny house, I was hungry for more room to spread out, hungry for some quiet and a little time to myself."

Macomber says she was also hungry to learn, which led to her enrollment in writing classes at a local college. She wanted to be a novelist so badly she could taste it. She kept writing and receiving rejections but soon came to realize that her deepest hunger was spiritual. She was reading scripture each morning. However, she acknowledged to herself that she was only skimming the surface of what it means to live a Christian life. Because she wanted more, wanted to go deeper in the Word, her "hunger" pushed her forward into seeking a deeper relationship with God.

A recent Facebook post by one of my former students touched my heart. Krista's husband is a police officer who has faced the horrors of teen suicide one too many times. Krista is now on a mission to educate young people that suicide is not the answer. I think Krista's word for the New Year is "mission."

As I have thought about, reread Macomber's magazine article, and responded to Krista's posts on Facebook, I chose "focus" for my New Year word. I have commented to several friends in the past months about my struggles to stay focused on God's leading because there are so many distractions in life. I have posted the word "focus" throughout my house on and my computer to remind me that my focus is on what He is doing through me and in my life.

Because it's so easy to allow the outside world to distract us from what is important in life, I challenge you to choose a word for the New Year. Macomber's past words have included trust, brokenness, prayer and hope. This year, she has chosen the word "listen."

If you feel led to explore the possibilities God has for your life, ask Him to reveal the word He has for you. When you trust Him, He will take you on a journey of discovery you never imagined.

What is your word for the New Year?

When You Remember Who Loves You

"Give thanks to the God of gods. His love endures forever"
—Psalm 136:2 (NIV).

The author of a recent morning devotional made me realize that I am not the only one who forgets, in my busyness, that I am loved by someone unconditionally. No matter the circumstances, when I turn to Him, I know I am forgiven, and I am loved, with no strings attached.

Before Jesus became my BFF or best friend forever, I worried too much about what others thought of me. How did they perceive my looks, my words, my shared thoughts and opinions, and my actions? Was I good enough to be a part of their circle?

Caught up in the things of this world, I craved other people's approval. I was addicted. Looking back, I can trace this need for approval to a mother who had good intentions but expected perfection from her daughters, who became what man defines as an over-achiever. I'm sure if I had known more about my mother's childhood and youth, I would have understood her better. Now, it doesn't matter. I knew she loved me and wanted the best for me, just like most parents, and just like our heavenly Father desires for us.

As I continue to grow spiritually, I have come to a new understanding and peace about my past, which has led me to forgive not only others, but myself, for mistakes that cannot be rectified except through grace. Just as His grace is a gift, we have to extend that gift to others, as well as ourselves.

Until I accepted that gift, I could not give it away. As someone once said, "You can't give away what you don't have."

How can we love another when we cannot accept the unconditional love that He has for us? I have to remind myself, as a parent, how I feel about my two sons and the lengths to which my love extends for their happiness. Isn't that how our heavenly Father feels about us?

In a recent sermon, my pastor said, "Life is hard, even for people of faith."

The following morning, a quote in a newspaper article on poverty, caught my attention: "Life is hard, but you can still be nice to each other."

Receiving what God has to offer, which is hard for some to believe and accept, is the only way to live, especially in today's world. His enduring love for us helps us to reach out to others in love, including the most unlovable of people.

I am sure that my past actions and words have made me unlovable in some people's eyes. I have to remind myself of that sometimes when I perceive others as unlovable. That's when I pray, "Please Lord, let me see that person through your eyes today."

It's only when we operate in God's love and put it into action that we become the person He created us to be. Remembering that His love endures forever is a message we need to share.

Are you sharing the message?

Doing the Next Right Thing

"Now all has been heard; here is the conclusion of the matter: Fear God and keep his commandments, for this is the whole duty of man"
—Ecclesiastes 12:13 (NIV).

Balancing my checkbook is not a pleasure for me. However, when I finish, I feel relieved when I find my math computations are not as far off as I thought. I have a love/hate relationship with numbers. Give me words any day.

A recent day found me going through my bank statement and checkbook register where I discovered a check for $30.36 that had not cleared, even though it had been almost a month. I picked up the phone and called the merchant in a nearby city to uncover the mystery of the missing check.

The puzzle was solved when the store manager checked records and video for that day and learned that the clerk, who had been in conversation with another employee, had returned my check, along with the receipt for the items I had purchased. Because I was used to other businesses who immediately return your check after providing a signature, I had not thought anything about the transaction. I had stuck the check and receipt in my purse until arriving home where I do what I always do with cancelled checks—I shredded it.

Without being asked by the manager, I offered to mail her a check for the amount I owed. She was quite surprised at my proposal and gave me the store mailing address.

Later that day, the topic of doing the right thing came up during a conversation with a close friend. She shared her story about a store clerk not charging her the correct amount for a purchase she had made. The error had been made in my friend's favor.

After leaving the store, she realized she had not been charged enough for the two hot dogs she had bought for a quick lunch. Because she was already on the road again and pressed for time, she waited until the next time she visited the store to bring it to a clerk's attention. When she insisted on paying for the second hot dog from the previous visit, he brushed it off with a "no big deal."

However, my friend persisted, replying, "It's not right." Eventually, the clerk, who was amazed by my friend's honesty, charged her the 99 cents plus tax for the food she had received in error.

~15~

When I, or someone I know, try to rectify a mistake that involves a business being short-changed, I am always amazed at the response. Although I wasn't always honest enough to return to the scene in the past, if I caught an error at the time, I would mention it to the clerk.

But returning days later to right a wrong is part of following God's commands. To fear God means to love Him and follow His ways. It means doing the next right thing. As followers of Christ, it is our duty to do just that, even if it means admitting we are wrong.

Are you doing the next right thing?

You Can't Hide

"Woe to those who go to great depths to hide their plans from the Lord, who do their work in darkness and think, 'Who sees us? Who will know?'"—*Isaiah 29:15 (NIV).*

When I read the news story about an 11-year-old boy who staged a hoax to cover up his bad grades, I had to chuckle. According to police, the boy faked his kidnapping to avoid bringing home a bad report card. The boy told authorities that a man with a pistol snatched him after he left Ed White Middle School, forced him into a "beat-up car" and threatened to kill him.

The youngster's story continued with his escape by jumping out of the car. However, he said he wasn't able to grab his backpack, which contained his report card. After running to his grandparents' house, the boy later confessed to lying. His grandfather called police to apologize.

Police were suspicious that the boy was able to "escape" with his band instrument, but not his backpack. The youngster has not been charged. However, I'm sure his parents or grandparents doled out the appropriate punishment for his creative lying.

In spite of the humor in this situation, the story stuck with me for two reasons: the lengths to which some people will go to hide things and my own past attempts to cover up the truth. As I thought about this young boy, I thought about a recent sermon that my pastor delivered on honesty and passing the buck. Recalling what happened in the Garden of Eden, we know that when Adam and Eve were caught doing what God had expressly forbid them to do, they hid from Him. Then, Eve passed the buck, blaming the serpent, and Adam blamed Eve for talking him into eating the off-limits fruit.

When we reflect on the Creation story and its meaning for us, we realize that, as my pastor says, it's our story too. We have all passed the buck at one time or another. Either we don't own up to the truth by fabricating an excuse or we blame it on someone else. It's much easier to do that than take responsibility. Eventually, however, we must pay the consequences of our choices.

I recall the times I tried to hide things from my parents. I usually was caught. Like most children, I wanted to avoid punishment. As my relationship with my heavenly Father has grown, I have learned you cannot hide anything from Him.

A simple, but profound, truth about Adam and Eve's choice in the garden is something I had never considered until my pastor's sermon on this topic. Another lesson we can take away from this story, he says, is learning that we need God and we must trust Him. How many times, though, do we take what we think is the easy way out, forgetting that the future is in His hands.

However, just like Adam and Eve, we've been saved by grace. In spite of the poor choices we make sometimes, we can be assured of His love.

Is there something you're hiding?

What's Holding You Back?

"Therefore God again set a certain day, calling it Today, when a long time later he spoke through David, as was said before: 'Today, if you hear his voice, do not harden your hearts'" *–Hebrews 4:7 (NIV).*

Do you know why the Procrastination Club still has no members? Because, if you have applied for admission, you don't qualify.

I had to laugh when I read this joke. Although I have never been known for letting grass grow under my feet, I've been guilty of putting some things off. Recently, I made a list of things I knew I needed to do but were not at the top of my priorities: change the filter in my home heating unit before winter, register my dog with the local animal control authorities (because it is a law) and set up an appointment to review insurance needs with my agent.

While none were an immediate concern for me, each time I viewed the list posted on my refrigerator door, it taunted me. I knew each needed to be taken care of in a timely manner. I would, however, glance at my list daily and talk myself out of doing the tasks that day. Finally, I made the decision to accomplish all three in one day. Once I had completed all three chores, I tossed the to-do list in the trash. The next day, however, I started thinking of more tasks that would need to be done in the near future. So, I started another list.

"USA Today" reported the following top five things people put off until the last minute: house chores/yard work, 47 percent of respondents; holiday gift shopping, 43 percent; making doctor/dentist appointments, 35 percent; calling relatives, 31 percent; changing oil in the car, 29 percent.

Why do we procrastinate? Different reasons apply, including indecision, perfectionism, fear, wounded pride and laziness, according to a "Psychology Today" report. However, there are also costs associated with putting things off, like wasted opportunities, the creation of problems and hurting others.

Christian writer Kay Arthur once said, "I am convinced beyond a shadow of any doubt that the most valuable pursuit we can embark upon is to know God."

Ten years ago, I realized what was holding me back from being my best. It was then that I began to pursue a relationship with my Creator. I grew up believing in Him but did not have a personal relationship.

~19~

Another Christian writer, Elizabeth Kubler-Ross, said, "It is only when we truly know and understand that we have a limited time on earth—and that we have no way of knowing when our time is up—that we will begin to live each day to the fullest, as if it were the only one we had."

In Luke 9:62, Jesus said, "No procrastination. No backward looks. You can't put God's kingdom off till tomorrow. Seize the day" *(The Message).*

Are you putting off an encounter with the living God until the last minute? Don't wait until life brings you to your knees.

Putting One Foot in Front of the Other

"When you walk, your steps will not be hampered;
when you run, you will not stumble"--*Proverbs 4:12 (NIV).*

In my mid-40s, the racing bug bit me after I began an exercise routine to lose weight. A friend and I became walking partners and on a lark, we entered our first 5K race. We had planned to power walk the 3.1 miles for fun. We weren't trying to win a trophy.

However, about a mile into the race, I was inspired, or should I say challenged, to start running by some of my high school students. More competitive than I realized, I couldn't let their "taunts" get the best of me. I finished third in my age division but not without paying the consequences. In addition to a trophy, I also earned shin splints because I was not wearing the proper footwear. Running shoes and walking shoes are designed differently.

Before entering the next competition, I did my research and purchased the correct shoes for running. It made a difference in the outcome. I earned a second place medal in the next race and was able to walk without pain afterwards.

Wouldn't it be nice if we could say the same about this journey called life? That it was as easy as making the right purchase to eliminate the pain. However, it's not that simple. We all have to make choices. Because we are each uniquely endowed by our Creator with different strengths, our life paths are different. However, sometimes we find ourselves at a crossroads in life, not certain which path to take. Fear of the unknown can stop us before we get to the finish line.

Think about Abraham who was called by God to leave his family. He left everything familiar to set out on a new journey in life. He had to make a choice to take that next step. Abraham left his comfort zone after placing his trust in God. He didn't have a detailed blueprint from God that revealed each leg of this new adventure but he took that next step.

Author C.S. Lewis says, "What saves a man is to take a step. Then another step."

Observe a young child who is just learning how to walk. He will cling to his parents' hands or a nearby object before he finally gains the courage to let go. Of course, he will fall many times before he is able to take several steps on his own. However, it is part of the process of letting go and taking that next step.

Sometimes, it requires more than a baby step. It takes a giant leap of faith as small as a mustard seed. Mustard seeds are tiny, about three millimeters in diameter. If you converted that into inches, it would equate to 0.1181. Can you find that on your ruler?

God doesn't ask us to stop and measure the distance but He does require us to take that next step. With faith and courage, we can put one foot in front of the other.

Are you ready to take the next step of faith?

Casting the First Stone

"Jesus bent down and wrote with his finger in the dirt. They kept at him, badgering him. He straightened up and said, 'The sinless one among you, go first: Throw the stone'"—John 8:6-8 (NIV).

I didn't recognize the woman's name on the return address label. When I opened the envelope, I discovered an 11-page handwritten letter from one of my column readers in another community. I always enjoy feedback from those who read my weekly column because it's affirmation that I am doing God's work. However, this letter has touched me more than some I have received because of its content.

As she poured out her feelings in blue ink on green paper, my heart ached for her. Although I have heard similar stories before, she had decided to share hers with me in writing. She has a past. We all do. We have all done things or said things that we regret. We are all sinners.

However, the words she wrote revealed a deeper pain, not due to her past, but because of the present. Although she knows God has forgiven her for her sins, people have not. In part, she said, "I haven't found a church that welcomes me."

As Christians, we sometimes wonder at the hatred spewed toward us. We often can't understand why anyone would not want to know Christ. Have you looked in the mirror lately and asked yourself, "Do my actions and words reflect a Christ-like attitude?"

Like many who have been turned off by the church, the writer of the letter has experienced the cold shoulder and gossip of those who profess to be Christians but merely show up to polish the same pew each week. Are you guilty?

In John 8, the Pharisees bring a woman caught in adultery before Jesus. Making her stand before the group, they said to Jesus, "Teacher, this woman was caught in the act of adultery. In the Law, Moses commanded us to stone such women. Now what do you say?"

Although they were looking for a way to trap Jesus and accuse Him, I am sure they did not expect His answer. Scripture says that Jesus bent down and started to write on the ground with his finger. Then, when they kept questioning Him, Jesus straightened up and said, "If any one of you is without sin, let him be the first to throw a stone at her." Again he stooped down and wrote on the ground.

Of course, since none of them was sinless, they walked away until only Jesus was left alone with the accused woman. The rest of the scripture reveals what we must take to heart. He then asked her, "Woman, where are they? Has no one condemned you?"

When she replied in the negative, Jesus declared, "Then neither do I condemn you."

Jesus' challenge in this passage should remind us to avoid judging others where there is sin in our own life that needs to be addressed.

Have you dropped your stone?

Get Vaccinated with Gratitude

"Enter His gates with thanksgiving and His courts with praise; give thanks to Him and praise His name"—*Psalm 100:4 (NIV).*

You can't turn on the television news or open a newspaper without hearing or reading another story about the economy. Some say the worst is over. Others believe it may take months or even years for a rebound. The economic downturn has impacted everyone. No one is immune.

According to a recent American Psychological Association survey of 7,000 households, 80 percent of Americans are stressed about the economy and their personal finances. Fifty-two percent reported lying awake at night worried about money. However, we can choose our response to this disturbing news by counting our blessings despite our circumstances. In his first letter to the Thessalonians (5:16-18), Paul wrote, "Be joyful always; pray continually; give thanks in all circumstances..."

Author and minister, Clinton C. Cox had this to say about thankfulness: "John Henry Jowett said, 'Gratitude is a vaccine, an antitoxin, and an antiseptic.' This is a most searching and true diagnosis. Gratitude can be a vaccine that can prevent the invasion of a disgruntled attitude. As antitoxins prevent the disastrous effects of certain poisons and diseases, thanksgiving destroys the poison of fault-finding and grumbling. When trouble has smitten us, a spirit of thanksgiving is a soothing antiseptic."

According to a study conducted several years ago by two researchers, Dr. Michael McCollough of Southern Methodist University, and Dr. Robert Emmons of the University of California, gratitude plays a big role in a person's well-being. Several hundred people participated in the study. While one group kept track in a journal of all the events that happened to them that day, another group noted only the bad experiences. A third study group wrote about those happenings for which they were grateful for each day. The findings revealed that the third group exhibited "higher levels of alertness, enthusiasm, determination, optimism and energy, and lower levels of depression and stress."

In his book, "Enough: Discovering Joy through Simplicity and Generosity," Pastor Adam Hamilton challenges his readers to take a notepad at the end of each day and write down five things for which they are thankful. Then, he says, thank God for these things. "Do this for sevendays, he says, "and see what happens as you cultivate the habit of giving thanks."

In her lifetime, author Melody Beattie, has survived abandonment, kidnapping, sexual abuse, drug and alcohol addiction, divorce and the death of a child. Still, she can say that "Gratitude unlocks the fullness of life. It turns what we have into enough, and more. It turns denial into acceptance, chaos to order, confusion to clarity. It can turn a meal into a feast, a house into a home, a stranger into a friend. Gratitude makes sense of our past, brings peace for today, and creates a vision for tomorrow."

Every day is an opportunity to count our blessings. There are 86,400 seconds in each one.

Have you used one of those seconds to say "thank you" to your Creator?

Is there a Cure for RHS?

"I have learned to be content with whatever I have. I know what it is to have little, and I know what it is to have plenty. In any and all circumstances, I have learned the secret of being well-fed and of going hungry, of having plenty and of being in need" *–Philippians4:11-12 (NIV).*

A bumper sticker caught my attention recently. It stated, "I brake for garage sales." I had to laugh because I've done the same thing. I don't stop at every garage sale I see and neither do I plan my Saturday around attending them. However, I know people who do.

Garage sales have grown in popularity. While there is nothing wrong with garage sales, I think they are a reflection of our consumer-driven culture. For example, have you ever found a new item in its original box at a sale? Or maybe you have discovered a new piece of clothing with the tags still attached. I know I have. What does that say about us as a society?

Our church members have been reading and discussing a book titled, "Enough: Discovering Joy through Simplicity and Generosity," by Adam Hamilton. In the book, Hamilton addresses the issues our country is currently facing, and it affects us all. As Hamilton says, Americans love their stuff.

We live in an instant-gratification world where credit card debt has skyrocketed, along with home foreclosures and even banks closing their doors. We have lost sight of what is important and have ceased to be content with the simple things in life.

Discontentment, says Hamilton, has led to a serious condition, much like restless leg syndrome in which one has twitches and contractions in the legs. The affliction that Hamilton is talking about, however, is called Restless Heart Syndrome (RHS). This syndrome is similar to RLS but it affects the heart or soul. The primary symptom of RHS is discontent. Never satisfied with what we have, we keep buying things trying to cure what ails us. If ignored, it can lead to destruction.

How many times have you purchased an item, only to lose interest or realize that it was not something you needed but thought you had to have? I'm certainly guilty.

While the apostle Paul was sitting in a Roman prison cell, he penned these words: "I have learned to be content with whatever I have. I know what it is to have little, and I know what it is like to have plenty."

Hamilton has visited Paul's prison cell in Rome where he discovered that the apostle had been lowered through a hole in the floor and dropped into a cavernous, damp pit. Yet, as Paul sat in that abyss, he found joy as he wrote his letter to the Philippians.

The Christmas season is here and many of us will spend more than we have trying to impress others or in an attempt to fill a void only Christ can. When we learn He is the only One who can quiet our restless heart, we can discover true joy.

Do you have RHS?

Join the Conspiracy

"From everyone who has been given much, much will be demanded; and from the one who has been entrusted with much, much more will be asked"–*Luke 12:48 (NIV)*.

Has the holiday season lost its meaning for you? Has it become a season of stress with traffic jams, shopping lists and the demands of finding the right gift for your loved ones? And what happens when it's all over? What happens when we're left with gifts to return because they aren't what we wanted or they don't fit?

What happens when we open the next credit card statement and see the looming debt that will take months, and sometimes years, to pay off? What happens when we stare into the emptiness after the twinkling lights have gone out and wonder, "What was that all about?"

What has happened to the season whose roots are in the birth of a baby who would grow up to radically change the world? His story, like no other, is one of promise, hope and a love we cannot even fathom in our wildest dreams.

What if Christmas became a world-changing event again? In 2006, five pastors decided to make Christmas a revolutionary event by encouraging their faith communities to "Worship Fully, Spend Less, Give More and Love All." With an overwhelming response to their collaborative efforts, Advent Conspiracy was born.

Advent Conspiracy has become a grassroots movement with more than 1,000 churches in 17 countries who are participating as co-conspirators to put meaning back into Christmas. Conspiracy projects are as varied as drilling a water well for those who lack access to clean water or simply encouraging congregations to think of meaningful acts of kindness to replace traditional gifts.

Last year, through Advent Conspiracy, $3 million was raised for relief projects which included providing clean water and medical attention in communities around the world. According to the "Conspiracy" website, the leading cause of death in under-resourced countries is a lack of clean water with 1.8 million people dying every year from water-borne illnesses. That includes 3,900 children a day.

While statistics reveal that Americans spent more than $450 billion on

Christmas last year, it costs only $10 to give one child clean water for life. Only $10.

What if each one of us decided that rather than giving a gift out of obligation, we committed to giving gifts that really will change the world? What if we gave quality time or donated to a worthy cause to provide clean water or food for the hungry? What if we looked for ways to be more loving, instead of fighting to be first in line to buy the latest popular toy that will end up broken or lost in the back of a child's closet?

The downturn in the economy has forced many of us in the U.S. to spend less. However, it's not just about saving money. It's about remembering that we are blessed to be a blessing.

Christmas can still change the world. Are you part of the conspiracy?

Getting Closer to God

"Give away your life; you'll find life given back, but not merely give back—given back with bonus and blessing. Giving, not getting, is the way. Generosity begets generosity"—*Luke 6:38 (MSG).*

My four-year-old grandson has begun to volunteer to say the blessing before each meal. Thanksgiving was no different and neither was his short but heartfelt prayer: "God is good. Amen."

While some might think that a prayer of thanksgiving should include more, it is a wonderful reminder that indeed, God is good. Sometimes, in our hectic days, especially now, we forget that He is good all the time.

Some have never accepted the gift that our heavenly Father gave each of us in the form of a small child born over 2,000 years ago. Even believers, who have failed to fully explore the blessings He offers, do not fully understand what it means unless they unwrap everything that the Father has for His children in Christ.

Until I opened the door of my heart over 10 years ago and said "Yes" to Jesus, I did not understand what it meant to be close to God. I grew up attending a small church in southwestern Louisiana. My sister and I actually walked a block from our house to attend Sunday school and church services. And even though, at age 14, I was baptized, I didn't understand what it meant to be fully committed to seeing life through His eyes.

As I have grown in my faith, trusting Him to guide me through the darkest of times, I have learned that He is always with me. As His word says, He has promised never to leave me or forsake me and He hasn't. I also know that, without Him, I would not have survived with grace, the events of the past 10 years, many of which brought me to my knees in prayer.

More importantly, growing closer to God has taught me that "it's not about me." As I have learned to be more generous with my time, talents and treasure, life has become more meaningful and my list of blessings grows daily.

I can remember seeing a billboard several years ago with the following quote: "If you don't feel as close to God as you used to, who moved?" It's so easy to get distracted by the things of this world and forget about what matters in life, especially during this time of year when we are urged to spend, spend, and spend some more.

However, if we choose to keep our focus on God, we will remember why we are celebrating this season. For when we recall what transpired over 2,000 years ago in a Bethlehem stable, we will be amazed once again at the wonder of His love for us imperfect humans.

And although we can't outgive God, we can learn from Him that giving, not getting, is the way to true blessings. When we cease to cling to riches, selfishness and greed, it is then that we truly draw closer to God.

Are you as close to God as you want to be?

What does a Miracle Cost?

"She will give birth to a son, and you are to give him the name Jesus, because he will save his people from their sins"—Matthew 1:21 (NIV).

My eyes must have been deceiving me. However, as I approached a popular convenience store and was able to see the sign more clearly, I knew there must be a mistake, or else it was a miracle. I was hoping for the latter. Gas had not been below a dollar in 10 years. But the bold numbers on the sign claimed 77 cents per gallon.

Entering the store to purchase a warm drink, I asked the store manager about the price. He confirmed my first thought upon seeing the sign, which was not working properly. I told him I knew it was too good to be true.

A recent news article, however, reminded me that miracles still happen. "Wrong Number Miracle" headlined the story about a mother, who was going to miss a mortgage payment if she sent money to a desperate daughter. It was the day before Thanksgiving and Lucy Crutchfield picked up the phone to let her daughter know that she would be sending money so the family could buy groceries. But Crutchfield dialed the wrong number. Instead of getting her daughter, she got Virginia Saenz, a real estate agent from a San Diego suburb. Crutchfield left a message but it was Saenz who responded. When Saenz heard the telephone message, she said, "It broke my heart."

Saenz did the only thing she could think of—she called Crutchfield back and told her not to worry. Crutchfield, who already had a money order prepared to make a mortgage payment, was going to cash it in to send money to her daughter. Saenz, however, told Crutchfield to keep her money and promised to take care of her daughter. And she did.

On Thanksgiving morning, Saenz and her 14-year-old son bought food for a Thanksgiving dinner and enough groceries to get Crutchfield's daughter through the end of the month—her next payday. Saenz said the act of giving made the day special for her and her son. "I think it's what anybody would have done," she added.

Our lives are filled with miracles. Although we are often too busy to notice them, they happen every day and our lives become richer. Christian author, Ruth Senter, once said, "The miracle of joy is this: It happens when there is no apparent reason for it. Circumstances may call for despair. Yet something different rouses itself inside us...We remember God. We remember He is love. We remember He is near."

The first Christmas was filled with extraordinary signs of God. The visits of angels, the star that guided Eastern wise men and the birth of a Savior over 2,000 years ago in a Bethlehem stable remind us of the greatest miracle. It's also a reminder of the price paid for that most special gift.

Unwrap that gift, cherish it and live with new purpose as we celebrate the birth of the One who came to save.

The Most Important Day of the Week

"Because of the Lord's great love we are not consumed, for his compassions never fail. They are new every morning; great is your faithfulness"—Lamentations 3:22-23 (NIV).

How would you respond if someone asked, "What's the most important day of the week?" If you replied "to-day," then you would be correct. Now, if you thought that was a trick question, think about this: "What are the two days of the week on which you should never worry?" One is yesterday and the other is tomorrow. It took over 40 years and probably closer to 50, for me to recognize this truth. After all, I am a work-in-progress.

Another truth I have come to embrace is God's promise that His mercies are new each morning. Recently, our pastor asked members of the congregation to raise their hands if God had ever given them a second chance. Quite a few hands were raised. Then, he asked for a show of hands from those who had been given three, four or more chances to start over. Again, hands shot up all over the room. My hand went up too.

I have lost count of the number of times I have stumbled. However, I have learned that with His grace, I don't have to stay down. His love brushes the dirt from the seat of my pants and, with His pat of encouragement on the back, I can begin anew. Beginning anew means accepting God's forgiveness and His extended hand. I can recall a time in my past when I would not have been able to do that. I did not feel worthy of His forgiveness. However, once I accepted His gift, I had to learn to forgive myself. And that was more difficult. A wise person once told me, "If our heavenly Father can forgive us, then we must honor Him by forgiving ourselves."

Although I have learned to forgive myself, I sometimes forget to ask God, as Psalm 139:24 says, "See if there is any offensive way in me." When I do, He usually brings to mind a transgression I have ignored. Until I deal with it, He continues to remind me. Nothing is so freeing, however, than to ask for forgiveness and, if necessary, to make right our wrongs.

Each morning before I get out of bed, I seek His face. As the words of Psalm 59:16 remind us, we should sing of His strength and His love each morning for He is our fortress and our refuge in times of trouble. Once we receive His new mercy, His comfort or new expression of love, we must share it with the world. When we do, it encourages us to press on while putting the past behind us. Even when we turn the calendar to a new day or a new year, it doesn't matter because God offers a fresh start each day.

Even when we hit bottom, all we have to do is look up and ask God for another chance.

Are You Exercising Your Faith?

"Have nothing to do with godless myths and old wives' tales; rather, train yourself to be godly. For physical training is of some value, but godliness has value for all things, holding promise for both the present life and the life to come"—*1 Timothy 4:7-8 (NIV).*

When I was younger, I never worried about gaining weight. I was a "skinny little thing," and at 5'3," weighed 98 pounds soaking wet when I graduated from high school in 1971. At one time, I could eat anything I pleased. Oh how I wish for those days.

However, age has caused my metabolism to slow down. When I was in my 40s, I began a serious exercise routine because as we grow older our muscle mass deteriorates and our bodies begin to decline if we don't take care of them. It requires exercise and eating healthy to maintain strength and energy.

Gym memberships increase after January 1 when people make New Year's Resolutions to get in shape. However, many often lose the drive to continue on the new routine after a few months. At the beginning, they are encouraged by the thoughts of "a new me." For some, it soon becomes drudgery if not done for the right reasons. Getting in shape requires desire, sacrifice and endurance to continue on the path to physical fitness.

So does exercising our faith. Just as we can't get physically fit by sitting on the couch, glued to the TV and munching on potato chips, we can't get spiritually fit by just attending church on Sunday. We aren't going to grow more Godly by osmosis. We have to learn to exercise our faith through effort. Author and missionary, Elisabeth Elliot, says, "Faith has to be exercised in the midst of ordinary, down-to-earth living."

Media messages bombard us daily with Chicken Little's message, "The sky is falling. The sky is falling." Instead of placing our faith in God, we place it in man. If we want to increase our faith, we have to take action, which means consciously ignoring the world's messages and concentrating on God's word. Jesus told His disciples, "I tell you the truth, if you have faith as small as a mustard seed, you can say to this mountain, 'Move from here to there' and it will move. Nothing will be impossible for you." Now, that's a strong faith, isn't it? Sometimes, I wish I had mustard seed faith.

Just as I exercise my body daily, I have to keep cultivating my faith. And when I recall His faithfulness in the past, it strengthens my trust in Him.

Another faith exercise I use is to begin each day with a picture of what God is doing in my life. I do this through prayer journaling. By praying and meditating about my day, I listen for His voice. Through this practice, I see His presence in every aspect of my life.

How strong is your faith? Does it need a little daily exercise? If we experience it regularly, we will find ourselves in the best spiritual shape of our lives.

If you can Relate, Raise your Hand

"…being confident of this, that He who began a good work in you will carry it on to completion until the day of Christ Jesus"
—Philippians 1:6 (NIV).

As my grown sons sat at my dinner table recently, our discussion turned to their childhood antics. We laughed as we recalled those instances when I considered going into the Witness Protection Program to escape or the times when I wanted to move and not leave a forwarding address. Sometimes, I still consider those options. If you are a parent and can relate, raise your hand.

My youngest celebrated his 29th birthday recently. As I see the man he has become, I smile because I know that God isn't finished with him yet. Neither is He finished with my firstborn. I also know that He still has much work to do in me and through me.

If you are following God, then you, too, are still one of His works-in-progress. Curious about that phrase, "work-in-progress," or WIP for short, I went online where I found the following definition in a Financial Dictionary at *Dictionary.com*: "Work that has not been completed but has already incurred a capital investment from the company."

If we think about WIP in terms of our spiritual maturity, the definition above makes even more sense. God has invested capital in us. He invested His Son, Jesus Christ, for our redemption. We don't have to do anything to earn it. However, we must say, "Yes," to Jesus and accept the gift of grace to save us from our own foolish pride that leads to sin.

If you can recall being a teenager and anticipating those magic numbers of 16, 18 and 21, you know that the days drag by slowly as you wait anxiously for each birthday to come so that you can get your driver's license, register to vote or consider yourself legally an adult. However, those numbers also come with a price—in one word: responsibility.

Another word for responsibility is accountability. When we choose to surrender our will to His, we are accountable for our spiritual growth. He has begun a good work in us but it is our responsibility to seek His guidance.

My sons don't always solicit my advice, even when I would give it so freely if asked. Maybe they are not ready to hear from someone whose wisdom has been hard earned and not without scars. However, I have learned through my own trials that I cannot teach them to trust God. I can only model what He has taught me.

I like this quote from comedian Jeff Foxworthy: "My kids have given me a glimpse of how God must feel. God looks at us, like, 'Oh, good grief, …you're driving me crazy, but I still love you.'"

Can you imagine how God felt when the Israelites kept going in circles for 40 years? He didn't give up on them and He doesn't give up on us.

When we realize His plan is better than any we could ever conceive, true spiritual growth begins.

Are You up to the Challenge?

"And whatever you do, whether in word or deed, do it all in the name of the Lord Jesus, giving thanks to God the Father through him"
–Colossians 3:17 (NIV).

At age 35, author Cami Walker was battling multiple sclerosis. Hospitalized for the depression that often accompanies the chronic neurological condition, making it difficult to walk, work, or enjoy life, she received a novel prescription from an African medicine woman: Give to others for 29 days.

"The first day of my personal '29-Day Giving Challenge' was preceded by a sleepless night," says Walker. "I was awake all night feeling angry and sorry for myself during a difficult flare up of my Multiple Sclerosis."

When insomnia hits, Walker often goes through old journals, reading notes that she's made. A note, from one of her spiritual teachers two months before, caught her attention. The note said, "Give something away each day for 29 days."

Although it was 3 a.m., Walker decided at that moment to take the suggestion. A simple supportive phone call to another friend living with MS was her first gift that next morning. Each day after that she woke up feeling excited about what she might give away that day. "I began to notice that the more I gave away, the more abundance I was experiencing for myself," she says. "I wanted to see what would happen in my life if I really committed and focused my energy on giving for 29 days."

However, in no way did she anticipate what unfolded because of her experiment. "By day 29, I was astounded by the magical and miraculous shifts in my energy for life. I was feeling happier, healthier, and more in awe with life. I found myself smiling and laughing more."

Walker did not plan her giving, but simply began her day, waiting to be moved to give something away. Her experiment became the basis for the insightful story, "29 Gifts," which documents the author's life change. Many of Walker's gifts were simple: a phone call, spare change, a Kleenex, a smile to a stranger.

These acts of generosity not only transformed Walker's life, but also led to the creation of her worldwide revival to encourage others to embrace a giving spirit. "I want to inspire more generosity on the planet and help change lives, one gift at a time."

As Walker learned, acts of giving don't even require money. When we give ourselves away, we learn it's also the only gift we get to keep. As Christian author Bette Reeves once said, "If you think you are too small to be effective, you have never been in bed with a mosquito."

To have a mosquito effect on others, you have to do something to change your world. In addition, when we set out to transform the lives of others, we leave a little part of ourselves behind.

Are you up to the challenge? Try it for the next 29 days and see what happens.

A Kiss from God

"O Lord my God, you have performed many wonders for us. Your plans for us are too numerous to list. You have no equal. If I tried to recite all your wonderful deeds, I would never come to the end of them"
—Psalm 40:5 (NLT).

If you're a parent, especially a mother, you understand the magic of a kiss when a young child comes to you with a minor bump, bruise or scrape. For some reason, kissing the injury provides miraculous healing in the eyes of the youngster. As a mother, I kissed many of my sons' skinned and banged up body parts. As a grandmother, I continue to use this unconventional medicine with my sons' children. I have never really understood why kissing a wound pacified the hurting one. However, it works most of the time with minor injuries.

In John 9, we learn of a man, blind since birth, who receives total healing from Jesus. This man's transformation is so dramatic he even looks different. Even the townspeople recognize the change. Most of us can recall this story but a recent Bible lesson we are studying in my Sunday school class revealed more. Jesus spat upon the ground and made clay of the spittle before anointing the man's eyes with the mixture. Although I had read this before, this lesson gave new insight. We might think it repulsive that Jesus used spit, but saliva has long been a folk remedy with ancient people believing strongly in its healing powers.

Although we might discount the healing power of a kiss to soothe a child's wound, we can't forget that our Lord is truly amazing. While we might be expecting big miracles, like healing from blindness, we often overlook His hug of blessings each day. Even in the bleakest winter landscapes of our lives, we can find some color if we will seek it.

In a recent sermon, our pastor shared the story of a woman who was so depressed about her life she sought counseling. After listening to the woman relate her problems, the counselor took out a prescription pad and wrote, "Go to the Grand Canyon."

Upon seeing the handwritten note, she questioned his antidote for her healing. The doctor's point? We need to get outside our own small world and ourselves to see the bigger picture that God has for us. Blinded by our own problems, we forget that God has bigger plans for our lives, plans too numerous to list. We also fail to remember He has already performed many wonders for us, and, as the psalmist says, if we tried to recite all His wonderful deeds, we would never come to the end of them.

Sometimes those sacred moments land on our nose as gently as a butterfly's wing while other times we need to look upward and reflect on His goodness. It is in times like these that we truly come to know the meaning of a kiss from our heavenly Father.

Has He kissed you lately?

Are You Living Life Backwards?

"You show that you are a letter from Christ, the result of our ministry, written not with ink but with the Spirit of the living God, not on tablets of stone but on tablets of human hearts"—*2 Corinthians 3:3 (NIV).*

For many years, I lived life backwards. Motivated by envy, I wanted what others had and I didn't. Caught up in what the world said I needed to be happy, I was lost until I came to understand the truth of what God has to offer His children. Because I have been there, I can relate when someone expresses unhappiness with his or her life. However, I have learned that when you are willing do what God asks, you will experience a life of fulfillment that money cannot buy. I didn't learn this lesson overnight or by osmosis. I had to live it.

I like this quote by Margaret Young, a popular singer and comedienne in the United States in the 1920s: "Often people attempt to live their lives backwards; they try to have more things, or more money, in order to do more of what they want, so they will be happier. The way it actually works is the reverse. You must first be who you really are, then do what you need to do, in order to have what you want."

The first step for me was discovering who I am in Christ. When I defined myself by other people's expectations, I had no clue who I really was. Therefore, I spent much of my life pleasing others and what I thought I wanted in life did not line up with God's Word. When I look back at where I was and where I am now, I am truly amazed at God's goodness. While I have been a wordsmith since I was old enough to pick up a pen, I never envisioned that I would be using my gift to glorify Him. However, when I trusted God's direction, He began to help me live life forward and to live it for Him.

Religious leader, Henry B. Eyring, once said, "Love is the motivating principle by which the Lord leads us along the way towards becoming like Him, our perfect example. Our way of life, hour by hour, must be filled with the love of God and love for others."

My friend, Sharon, loves to share her testimony of living in a fog for too many years. Her history includes childhood abuse and an alcoholic husband. However, God has turned her mess into a message. Recently, during an afterschool church program, she had decorated the classroom for Valentine's Day. Excited, the children asked why she had done so much for them. When she replied, "It's a ministry for me," she also asked them if they knew the definition of ministry.

One wise seven-year-old responded, "It's like a little door opens in your heart and lets you know that you love someone and you want to serve them."

I think this youngster has it figured out. Don't you?

Have You Allowed Him to Claim Your Life?

"Still other seed fell on good soil. It came up and yielded a crop, a hundred times more than was sown. When he said this, he called out, 'He who has ears to hear, let him hear'"--*Luke 8:8 (NIV)*.

A recent conversation with an acquaintance reminded me of how our Heavenly Father works in our lives. An avid gardener, Mary, was sharing some of her secrets when she told me about her mother's phone call during a recent winter snow. She asked her daughter, "Did you throw out your poppy seeds?"

Poppy seeds in the snow? Amazed, I asked for more information. Mary explained that she purchases packages of inexpensive mixed seeds and scatters them in her flowerbeds. She doesn't cover them up with soil. Whatever seed the birds don't eat proliferate into beautiful blooms each spring, summer and fall.

In the spring of 1968, at the age of 14, I was baptized. I didn't recall the date until I discovered my Certificate of Baptism while searching for my birth certificate in early 2008 so I could apply for a passport. Forty years after my baptism, I was preparing for my first mission trip to a foreign country. While I grew up in the church, I had no idea I was missing the most important relationship we can ever embrace in our lives. In October 2001 on a quiet Sunday afternoon by the lake, I rededicated my life to the Lord. As I have watched Him work in my life and the lives of my loved ones, I thank Him that He never gave up on me.

Just as the farmer prepares the ground, sows seed, waters and then must wait for the crop, we have to remember that producing a crop is a process over time. Bearing fruit does not happen overnight. I was reminded of this when my two oldest grandchildren were baptized recently. While they are too young to understand the true significance, seeds have been planted. It's the beginning of a lifelong journey of faith as they seek to grow and are guided by their church community.

On March 19, 2010 I remembered my baptism in the Jordan River. Jesus was on a mission when He came from Galilee to the Jordan seeking to be baptized by John. Although John tried to deter Him, Jesus insisted, "Do it. God's work, putting things right all these centuries, is coming together, is coming together right now in this baptism."

I never dreamed I would have the opportunity to walk where my Savior walked. As a teenager, I had solemnly covenanted with the help of God to turn from all sin and to accept Jesus Christ as Savior and Lord. I have failed many times in my life. I am not perfect. However, I have been made new through the birth of baptism. I celebrated my rebirth by remembering I have "put on Christ," and allowed Him once again to renew His claim on me.

Have you allowed Him to claim your life?

Have You Found Your Purpose?

"It's in Christ that we find out who we are and what we are living for. Long before we first heard of Christ and got our hopes up, He had his eye on us, had designs on us for glorious living, part of the overall purpose He is working out in everything and everyone"—*Ephesians 1:11-12 (MSG)*.

A website I came across recently proclaimed the following: "How to Finally Find Your Purpose!" Curious, I checked out the claim. According to the authors, "If you feel stuck, unhappy or overwhelmed in your career or life, we know just what you need." They also offer ways to get unstuck, including an eight-step life plan. I liked some of the suggestions. However, after reading much of the website, I realized one important factor was missing—God's plans.

Like many self-help authors, these writers overlooked one of the most important aspects of our lives—learning the reason for your being. Did you know that you were born with a God-given purpose? If you didn't know that, you are not alone.

Minister Gillis Triplett offers these six Bible verses to affirm our reason for being:

- Every human being entered into the earth realm with a God-given purpose (Ecclesiastes 3:1).
- No man or woman ever born came without a God-given purpose (II Timothy 1:9).
- Everyone was born with gifts, talents and abilities to assist them in fulfilling their God-given purpose (Romans 11:29).
- It is the responsibility of each individual to learn his or her God-given purpose (Romans 12:2).
- You must be able to convey your God-given purpose to others, (Habakkuk 2:2).
- If you fail or refuse to learn your God-given purpose, your options automatically become: (a) your own personal vision for your life, (b) society's vision for your life, or (c) the devil's vision for your life. With these plans, you may experience great financial success, but in the end, none of these visions will bring you fulfillment, satisfaction or peace of mind (Proverbs 19:21).

When I taught high school, I observed that some students chose careers based on potential earnings in a field. However, many dropped out of college or changed their majors more than once because they did not understand that, prior to birth, God placed in each one of us the necessary gifts, talents and abilities that we would need to fulfill His purpose for our life.

Playwright George Bernard Shaw wrote: "This is the true joy in life, the being used for a purpose recognized by yourself as a mighty one; the being thoroughly worn out before you are thrown on the scrap heap; the being a force of nature instead of a feverish selfish little clod of ailments and grievances complaining that the world will not devote itself to making you happy."

Another author, Erma Bombeck, said, "When I stand before God at the end of my life, I would hope that I would not have a single bit of talent left, and could say, 'I used everything you gave me.'"

I hope I will be able to say the same. Will you?

Are You Still Searching?

"They found the stone rolled away from the tomb, but when they entered, they did not find the body of the Lord Jesus"
—*Luke 24:2-3 (NIV)*.

"Who will roll the stone away from the entrance?" According to the gospel of Mark, this was the question that three women, Mary Magdalene, Mary the mother of James, and Salome, pondered as they took their spices to anoint their beloved Jesus' body at the tomb. However, when the three arrived, they saw that the stone, "which was very large, had been rolled away."

Instead, an angel greeted the women. He said, "Do not be afraid, for I know that you are looking for Jesus, who was crucified. He is not here; he has risen, just as he said. Come and see the place where he lay. Then go quickly and tell his disciples: 'He has risen from the dead and is going ahead of you into Galilee. There you will see him.' Now I have told you."

Can you imagine the thoughts racing through these women's minds and the conversation they had as they raced to find the disciples? It was a day they would never forget. Scripture tells us the three departed quickly from the tomb. They didn't hang around debating the issue but "with fear and great joy ran to tell the disciples."

On the way to spread the news, the three women are astonished to meet the risen Christ. Falling at His feet, they worship Him. He tells them, "Do not be afraid. Go and tell my brothers to go to Galilee; there they will see me."

Arriving in Galilee, the disciples also experienced the resurrected Christ. Matthew 28:17 says, "...when they saw him they worshiped him; but some doubted." Today, many people still doubt because they have not experienced the joy that comes from knowing the risen Savior.

On a pilgrimage to Israel, I experienced many holy sites, including the two suggested locations where Jesus was crucified, buried and rose from the grave. One site, the Church of the Holy Sepulchre, embraces within its walls the traditional tomb of Christ. Another site, promoted by General Charles Gordon, a British military leader in the 19th century, is located on a rocky hillside and has become known as the Garden Tomb. Both places are beautiful in their distinct ways, but archaeological evidence points to the Church of the Holy Sepulchre as the traditional site.

For some, like me, the place is not important because the death and resurrection of our Savior doesn't depend on the location of an authentic site. Our search is over because we won't find His body in any grave. The words to this 1933 hymn by Alfred H. Ackley say it all:

He lives, He lives,
Christ Jesus lives today!
He walks with me
and talks with me along life's narrow way.
He lives, He lives,
salvation to impart!
You ask me how I know He lives?
He lives within my heart.

Does He live in your heart? It's the best place of all.

Will You Surrender?

"…I have come that they may have life, and have it to the full"
—John 10:10 (NIV).

If you've ever been away from home for an extended period, you can understand the strangeness of walking into your house for the first time upon your return. After being away 10 days from my Oklahoma home, my eyes, as well as my other senses, had to adjust to what had once been familiar.

Eight of those 10 days were on holy ground where I inhaled the sights, sounds, tastes, smells and textures of another culture so foreign to this country girl that I had to pinch myself several times before I was aware of my surroundings. Israel, the Holy Land, so beautiful and richly steeped in history and a focal point for some of the most dramatic events that mankind has ever known.

Jesus was born there. He grew up there. He fulfilled his prophecy, met his death and ascended to heaven in this narrow strip of land. The topography was not what I expected. Pictured in my mind's eye was a sea of deserts. Instead, my camera captured vistas of towering mountains, lush green valleys, desert cliffs and turquoise waves lapping against the shore.

Our first full day in Israel dawned with a view of the Mediterranean from the hotel balcony. As far as I could see was a body of water whose name, derived from the Latin *mediterraneus*, means "in the middle of the earth." I was there as my mind pictured a boat on the horizon seen dimly through the early morning fog. Our pastor had suggested the previous evening that we rise early and imagine Jonah on that boat trying to run away from God. Can anyone escape God, even in a sea of 965,000 square miles?

I wondered, as I stared out over the miles and miles of wind-driven waves, how it would feel to try to outrun God. I knew how Jonah must have felt. I, too, had tried to run away from my Heavenly Father at one time. It is futile.

Now, I had traveled thousands of miles to places I had only read about in the Bible. I didn't feel a need to escape but had a hunger to know more and to experience what those who had gone before me had endured for their faith. Ruins, more than 2,000 years old, echoed their footsteps.

After returning home, I still close my eyes and recall the sound of waves lapping against the side of the wooden boat as we drifted in the Sea of

Galilee. Jesus walked across the same water toward His disciples. Peter, the bold one, left the boat, confident in his own abilities as he attempted to walk toward his teacher. I can imagine Peter's fear when he took his eyes off Jesus and began to sink. He cried out, "Lord, save me!"

These three small, but powerful words invite Him to be the Lord of our lives. He longs for an intimate, personal relationship with you.

Will you surrender?

Where's the Delete Button?

"If you put your trust in the love of Jesus Christ, your sins are wiped out, 'There is no condemnation for those who belong to Christ'"
—Romans 8:1 (NLT).

Being able to compose your thoughts in a word-processing program is nice. You can let the words flow and then edit afterwards. However, if you are old enough to remember what it was like to do timed drills on an old-fashioned typewriter, you can really appreciate today's technological advances.

I was the fastest typist in my high school class and the machines were manual. To correct a mistake, we had to use a special eraser brush. You will probably only find them in the Smithsonian now, both the typewriter and the correction tool.

The delete button on my computer keyboard probably gets the most workout. Although I try to refrain from editing while I am composing, I am my own worst critic and find myself, in spite of the advice I give to fledgling writers, stopping to read what I have written before I have finished the entire piece.

Recently, I read the following story that Pastor Rick Warren of Saddleback Church, shared in a daily devotional. He said, "I've got a friend named Buddy who says, when he was a little kid, his Sunday school teacher taught him that God was sitting in heaven writing down every bad thing that Buddy ever did. Writing it down! She actually made the class sing a song every week that went: 'My Lord is writing all the time. Writing, writing, writing all the time.' Buddy says, "It scared me. I just thought, 'I am never going to make it to heaven. My list is getting longer and longer.'"

Now, if that were true, none of us would make it into heaven. I know I wouldn't. I don't like to look back at my dumb mistakes and the poor choices I have made. Occasionally, I still make them because I ignore that still, small voice. In the past, there were times God had to hit me over the head with a 2 x 4 to get my attention, and it was not pleasant.

Each day is an opportunity to place our faith in Him, and recall that His death and resurrection releases us from judgment. John 3:18 says, "There is no judgment against anyone who believes in him. But anyone who does not believe in him has already been judged for not believing in God's one and only Son."

My pastor's recent sermon was titled "Practicing Easter." One of the points he made concerned periods of spiritual dryness in our lives. Pastor Ray said, "We must pray for resurrection, not resuscitation, because we need to seek new possibilities and new opportunities in our lives."

In that spirit, we must realize that putting our faith in Christ means God is not keeping a written list of our mistakes, but as Pastor Warren says, "He is erasing, erasing, erasing, all the time. Forgiving, forgiving, forgiving all the time. He's sitting in heaven hitting the delete button."

Aren't you grateful for His amazing grace?

What's in Your Field?

He replied, "Because you have so little faith. I tell you the truth, if you have faith as small as a mustard seed, you can say to this mountain, 'Move from here to there' and it will move. Nothing will be impossible for you"
–Matthew 17:20 (NIV).

Mustard seed faith. You've probably heard this expression more than once. I've heard it many times but I never really understood until I purchased some mustard seeds while I was in Israel several years ago. I, along with others on the trip who had never seen one, was amazed at how tiny they are. According to various websites I searched, a mustard seed is about 3mm in diameter or the size of the end of a sharpened pencil lead.

Looking at those tiny seeds and thinking about the point that Jesus was trying to make in His parable, I wondered, "Do I have that kind of faith?" When I look back at the prayers He has answered, and some He has left unanswered, I wonder what was different about the prayers. Was my faith stronger at the times He answered a prayer? Did I give up too soon when prayers went unanswered? Were they just not part of God's plan for my life or was it a combination of both?

Regardless of the answer, I know that trusting Him results in more faith, even in the darkest of times. Sometimes, it seems that the bad stuff won't take a break and we can lose hope. However, if you were to look at a tiny speck of mustard seed in the palm of your hand, and recall His words in Matthew, you might realize the power of that kind of faith. Matthew 13:32 says, "Though it is the smallest of all your seeds, yet when it grows, it is the largest of garden plants and becomes a tree, so that the birds of the air come and perch in its branches." I saw those garden plants in Israel and was amazed at the large bush that grew from such a minuscule seed.

A friend and I were discussing that type of faith recently, when she said, "I have come to realize that the mountains Jesus was talking about were the burdens that we carry around on our shoulders that we have not yet released to Him."

Author Virginia Pearce said, "We all know that more faith won't make our problems disappear. But I believe as our faith increases, we become more able to not only survive the hard times but become better because of them. I believe faith is the answer."

Another author, Mary Adams, shared this overheard conversation between two farmers: "I planted some grain last year. The seed sacks said that they contained 99 percent grain, but one percent 'other seeds.' Now I had no idea that the 'other seeds' were mustard seeds, and when I went to harvest that field...I was shocked! The one percent mustard seeds had taken over my entire field!"

What about your faith? Has it taken over your entire field?

Have You Been Telling Stories?

"We will not hide them from their children; we will tell the next generation the praiseworthy deeds of the Lord, his power, and the wonders he has done"—*Psalm 78:4 (NIV)*.

A recent lunch conversation with some friends reminded me of the importance of sharing our stories. My friend, Phyllis, related a story from her childhood of hiding underneath a large bush. However, she didn't realize she was sitting in the middle of an ant mound. When the ants started crawling inside her clothes, she ran to the house screaming, "I've got ants in my pants."

Phyllis has shared this story with her children as well as nieces and nephews who, she says, love hearing the story again and again. Those of us who survived our childhood have many tales to relate, some humorous, some terrifying, some sad, some embarrassing. Some, we never reveal.

What if these famous people had never shared their stories? A teacher told Thomas Edison that he was too stupid to learn. Walt Disney was fired from his job at a newspaper because his editor said he didn't have any creative ideas. Beethoven's music teacher told him he had no hope as a composer.

What do these three have in common? They told their stories or we would never have experienced the inspiration of their determination to succeed. Everyone has a story to share but the most important one we need to communicate is the day we gave our life to Christ. It is the most influential way to pass on to everyone, including our children, the "praiseworthy deeds of the Lord, His power, and the wonders He has done."

Many Christians feel a need to stand on the street corner and thump people over the head with the Bible. Do they expect to teach by osmosis or maybe beat it into their brains?

It is by our example, as we learned from Jesus, that we are able to share the good news. How many times in scripture does Jesus heal the blind, the lame, and the ill only to have the grateful benefactor start shouting for joy and spreading the word of His love for us?

Think of the crippled man whom Jesus healed by the pool of Bethesda. For 38 years, this man had lain by the pool, waiting for his turn to get in the famous waters of healing. However, Jesus told him to pick up his mat and walk. Wow, what a story he had to tell others. He couldn't keep that news to himself and why would he want to?

Since Jesus became Lord of my life, I have had no trouble sharing what He has done for me and through me. I am humbled by His grace. When a conversation lends itself to telling my story, I tell of the extreme makeover I have received. It is also a reminder for me of His love. He never abandoned me. I was the one who walked away.

Have you walked away from God? Do you need a reminder of His love? Who needs to hear your story?

Throw Away Your Guilt Kit

"All the prophets testify about him that everyone who believes in him receives forgiveness of sins through his name"—*Acts 10:43 (NIV)*.

If you're a mom, or can remember your mother doing the following, then you can appreciate these words I read on a coffee mug recently: "Mom, I'll always love you but I'll never forgive you for cleaning my face with spit on a hanky!"

I had to laugh aloud because I have been on both ends, the receiving and the giving. However, I didn't use a hanky. I used my hand and I can still remember my sons ducking when they saw me wetting my fingertips to wipe their face or slick down a wild cowlick.

Mothers probably carry around more guilt than most. When our adult children make poor choices, we start examining what we did wrong as the person who carried and nourished the new life for nine months in our body. I think that might be the reason we tend to accept their failures as our failures. They were literally connected to us through the umbilical cord that provided everything necessary for their growth and survival.

Most of us can relate to feelings of guilt at one time or another in our lives. In addition, some of us find it hard to forgive ourselves for the bad choices we have made. I was amazed by the following story as told by Steve Goodier:

"I read of a New Jersey artist who capitalized on people's need to let go of the past by selling them 'guilt kits.' Each kit contained 10 disposable brown paper bags and a set of instructions which said, 'Place bag securely over your mouth, take a deep breath and blow the guilt out. Dispose of bag immediately.' Amazingly, 2,500 kits sold at $2.50 each. But perhaps not so amazing when you think of the guilt many of us carry around."

In "The Capitol of the World," a short story by Ernest Hemingway, a Spanish father seeking reconciliation with his son, places a newspaper ad that reads, "Paco, meet me at Hotel Montana noon Tuesday. All is forgiven." When the father arrives, he is astounded to find 800 young men named Paco waiting for their fathers.

While we can never underestimate the need for forgiveness and restoration to wholeness, I have learned that the true path to letting go of guilt and seeking forgiveness must begin with accepting Christ as our Savior.

In Lee Strobel's "The Case for Easter," the investigative journalist writes about his search to find evidence for the resurrection. When Strobel, a former atheist, sets out to distinguish fact from myth, he didn't know he would eventually find the real truth. At the end of his journey, he said, "Because of the evidence, I now believed Jesus to be the Son of God. But to become his child, it was necessary for me to receive the free gift of forgiveness that he purchased with his life on the cross."

You don't need to buy a guilt kit. Just say "yes" to Jesus.

Have you accepted His gift?

What's the Best Advice?

"Listen to advice and accept instruction, and in the end you will be wise"
—*Proverbs 19:20 (NIV).*

"You'll shoot your eye out." If you've ever watched the classic movie "A Christmas Story," you might be able to relate to Ralphie who was trying to convince his parents to buy him a Red Ryder BB gun as a gift. In the 1940s, the Red Ryder was a popular boy's toy.

We can all remember similar advice from our parents like "wash behind your ears," "do unto others," "bundle up or you'll catch a cold," and the list could go on.

Our elders love giving advice. However, it doesn't stop there. We are bombarded daily with advice on talk shows, like Dr. Phil and Oprah, to the evening news bytes, giving us health warnings. Those warnings aren't necessarily bad either.

When was the last time you found yourself offering what you considered helpful advice to someone else but he or she did not take it that way? If you care about others and hate to see them troubled, it is hard to refrain from giving what we feel is "friendly" advice.

If you're a parent, you're probably also prone to giving advice, especially when you see your grown children making mistakes. I can recall advice I received from my parents when they were still alive. I can also look back at the poor choices I have made and the advice I did not take because I thought I knew better. I have concluded that those who are older are, for the most part, wiser. That is because they have lived what younger people are experiencing.

Ecclesiastes 1:9 says, "What has been will be again, what has been done will be done again; there is nothing new under the sun."

Although we live in a rapidly changing world often defined by the latest technology gadget, people have not changed. Study scripture and you will find story after story of those who did not heed the advice given by prophets in the Old Testament.

The New Testament, as well, offers a wealth of admonitions and exhortations for those who would follow it. The parables of Jesus and his Sermon on the Mount offer the best advice. To those who, as He says in Mark 4:9, have "ears to hear, let him hear."

Much of the time, we brush off well-meant advice because, as an old saying goes, "Advice would always be more acceptable if it didn't conflict with our plans."

Proverbs 19:21 says, "Many are the plans in a man's heart, but it is the Lord's purpose that prevails."

Two female centenarians, recently interviewed for a newspaper article, were receiving a free hair-and-makeup session at a local upscale salon. At the end of the interview, the reporter asked one of the women if she had any advice to offer for living to 100. She replied, "Just leave it to God. He paves the way."

That's the best advice I've ever heard. Don't you agree?

Searching in All the Wrong Places

After the earthquake came a fire, but the Lord was not in the fire. And after the fire came a gentle whisper. When Elijah heard it, he pulled his cloak over his face and went out and stood at the mouth of the cave. Then a voice said to him, "What are you doing here, Elijah?" —*1 Kings 19:12-13 (NIV).*

Searching for a clean page in the small notebook I always carry with me, I came across a scribbled message to myself. I carry the spiral pad with me to jot down writing ideas I don't want to forget. My handwriting, not as neat as it used to be, was still legible. The words, written while waiting to meet a friend for lunch, were a reminder from God.

As I read what I had written the previous fall, a mind picture returned as if captured with my camera. I was sitting on the front porch swing at a local restaurant known for its unique atmosphere and delicious cuisine. It is in the heart of our city and close to the hustle and bustle of life and the shrill whistles of the trains passing through about every 30 minutes, or so it seems. However, that day, God knew I needed a respite from the cacophony of life. While waiting for my friend, I was enjoying the breeze that rustled the leaves of nearby trees.

Savoring a moment away from the stresses of daily life, I heard an owl declaring his presence in the midst of man's chaos and unexpectedly, in the middle of a sunny day. For me, it was a welcome sign from my Lord and a reminder that He is always present if we will only seek His face.

In 1 Kings 19:11-13, the prophet Elijah was searching for God. However, he didn't find Him in the wind, an earthquake or a fire. He found God in a gentle whisper. Sometimes, it is hard to believe in what can't be seen. We search and we search, looking for the spectacular, like an earthquake, to jolt us out of our mundane lives instead of accepting what God has to offer us, like the hoot of an owl.

We might crave His presence at our breakfast table with a detailed list of instructions for our lives. We might think, "If God could speak directly to Abraham, Moses, Elijah, Mary or the apostle Paul, why won't He talk to me?"

Is it because we don't take the time to nurture the Spirit of His truth? In our busy lives, do we forget to let Him come alive in our hearts? Do we ignore or not seek His guidance and demand our way, rather than saying, "Your will be done."

In Jeremiah 29:13, the Lord says, "You will seek me and find me when you seek me with all your heart." God's will is best for us and it is His dream for our lives. When we quit wanting more *from* God, and began seeking more *of* God, then the real adventure begins.

Are you seeking more of Him?

You've Got 86,400 Seconds

"But your hearts must be fully committed to the Lord our God, to live by his decrees and obey his commands, as at this time"—*1 Kings 8:61 (NIV)*.

I am in the latter half of my fifth decade. Recently, I told a friend that even if I had several hundred years to live, I would never be able to reach all of the goals I have set for myself. I realize, however, that my goals may not be the same as God's plans for my life, and I'm okay with that.

The following poem, often recited by Dr. Benjamin Elijah Mays, is about squeezing value out of the time God has given each of us. We often forget, however, that our time on earth is a gift from our Heavenly Father. It is for our use, but it is limited to the number of days we live.

I've only just a minute,
Only sixty seconds in it.
Forced upon me, can't refuse it,
Didn't seek it, didn't choose it,
But it's up to me to use it.
I must suffer if I lose it,
Give an account if I abuse it,
Just a tiny little minute,
But eternity is in it.

Born in 1894 to former slaves, Mays was inspired by Frederick Douglas, Paul Laurence Dunbar and Booker T. Washington. He became a Baptist minister, earned a Ph.D. from the University of Chicago, served as Dean of the Howard University School of Religion, was an advisor to several United States presidents, served as a member and as President of the Atlanta Board of Education, and was President of Morehouse College for 27 years. In addition to his own vast accomplishments, Mays was an inspiration and advisor to his students, including Dr. Martin Luther King, Jr., who referred to Dr. Mays as his "spiritual mentor."

Dr. Mays, commenting on our mission, said, "All around you in this broken world, people are suffering. So many unmet needs exist that it can all seem overwhelming. But it's not naïve to think that you can make a significant and lasting difference for the better. As a Christian, God calls you to do so, by representing Jesus in the world. God doesn't intend for you to shrink back from the needs around you; He wants to use your life to help others. In fact, God has uniquely created you to meet certain needs and is hoping you'll accept your mission."

To accomplish our mission, we must imagine our day as a bank account. If we are credited each morning with $86,400, but it carries over no balance from day to day, and every evening cancels whatever amount we have failed to use during the day, we'd draw out every cent. Everyone has such a bank account but it's credited with time, 86,400 seconds every morning. Every night it writes off, as lost, whatever of this time you have failed to invest to good purpose.

As each year passes, I feel the urgent need to invest my time wisely.

Are you spending your 86,400 seconds carefully?

The Freedom to be Okay

"Then you will know the truth, and the truth will set you free"
—John 8:32 (NIV).

"*How* do you become okay with yourself?" How would you answer that question?

A young woman who is going through a difficult time posed this question to me recently. Before I set my eyes upon Jesus, I could not have answered her.

Growing up during the 60s, I never felt I was okay, at least by society's standards. According to the dictionary, the word okay has the following meanings: all right, satisfactory, acceptable and adequate. Even as an adult, I had a hard time accepting myself, faults and all. Things changed in my late 40s when I began searching for something to fill the emptiness that had once been filled by doubts, fear and a need to please. That something was Jesus.

Before I began seeking to please God, I worked hard at pleasing people. I wasn't honest with others about who I really was, and instead presented an image of who I thought I *should* be in order to gain acceptance. As that hole inside of me grew, I became more and more unsure of who I really was. Confused, I cried out to God one day. When His peace began to fill me, I knew I was finally learning the true meaning of freedom.

Author Brennan Manning writes, "We give glory to God simply by being ourselves." However, we can't be ourselves if we don't even know who we are in Christ.

Recently, I purchased a Wii Fit because I like to have fun with my exercise. Trying the step aerobics, I became annoyed when the word "okay" would pop on the screen because my steps were not quite on target. However, if I were on the mark with my steps, the word "perfect" would pop up in bold letters. Being a little competitive and a recovering perfectionist, I found myself trying to concentrate on my feet instead of the figure I was supposed to be following on my television screen. Consequently, I lost focus and began to miss steps because I was determined to be more than "okay."

When we take our eyes off the One who created us and place our focus on society's standards of what is acceptable, we are not living up to Christ's greatest command: Love your neighbor as yourself. This assumes a love of self. However, liking yourself isn't arrogant or self-centered. Instead, it's accepting the Creator's gifts and valuing yourself as Christ values you.

Looking to others for affirmation that you are okay only leads to frustration and disappointment. And human beings will disappoint you. 1 Corinthians 13:12 says, "Now we see but a poor reflection as in a mirror; then we shall see face to face. Now I know in part; then I shall know fully, even as I am fully known."

God alone is our true mirror. If we are free in Christ to be who we are, then it's more than okay to be less than perfect.

Finding Freedom in the Simple

"Command them to do good, to be rich in good deeds, and to be generous and willing to share"—*1 Timothy 6:18 (NIV)*.

"But how will he learn to share?" These were the words from my four-year-old grandson, commenting on his 10-month-old cousin's status as an only child. Brennan, who has an older sister, has learned through trial and error that he has to share. However, my second oldest grandchild also has a sweet spirit and a giving nature. He was also concerned that his cousin would not learn the meaning of sharing without having a sibling.

World-renowned evangelist Billy Graham once said, "We are not cisterns made for hoarding, we are channels made for sharing." Graham's comment is never more relevant than in today's society of "big and more" is better. I was astounded to read about a billionaire's mansion that is on the market for $75 million, despite the fact that construction has not been completed. What is even more astonishing is what the 90,000 square foot home includes: 13 bedrooms, 23 bathrooms, 10 kitchens, a 20-car garage, three swimming pools, a two-story wine cellar, a roller rink and bowling alley.

The home, advertised as a "monument to unparalleled success," is not far from Tiger Woods' home but is much larger. While there have not been any known offers on the home, it boasts 1,250 square feet of water front property and 68,000 square feet of climate-controlled housing. News reports speculate why the unfinished luxury home is on the market. However, I wonder why anyone would want a house that is the size of a mini mall in the first place.

By contrast, a friend recently wrote about her observations on an ordinary Friday. To the casual observer, she said, it might seem typical for a woman reading a book by her favorite author. However, for my friend, it was much more than that. For her, it was a gift from God as the book's theme centered on a beach, reminding her of younger days where she grew up near the ocean.

"Imagine my joy when I read about the beach and sea shells, sea glass and sand dollars," she said. "They are God's treasures."

"Have you ever thought," she added, "of how He protects them, how they are tossed by the sea, turned by the waves and left on the sand where people handle them and collect them, and no matter their size, they arrive intact, perfect, and one more time we are blessed by His creations. They are gifts to human hands and eyes."

Continuing with her observations, her email read, "Life is a treasure of blooming flowers, bird calls and more…treasures heaped on us daily, too many to count, big and small, maybe insignificant, but mighty in the grand scheme of things."

Her thoughts were a reminder of how freedom in this life is found in the simple things of everyday life and not million-dollar mansions. It's also about sharing with others what He has given us.

Have you found freedom in the simple?

Don't Worry Your Prayers

"If you don't know what you're doing, pray to the Father. He loves to help.
You'll get his help, and won't be condescended to when you ask for it. Ask
boldly, believingly, without a second thought. People who 'worry their
prayers' are like wind-whipped waves. Don't think you're going to get
anything from the Master that way, adrift at sea, keeping all your options
open"— *James 1:6-8 (MSG).*

Recently, a friend shared her prayers and revelation concerning her adult
children and grandchildren, who were traveling to Mexico to visit family.
The two adults and three children had set out on their journey around 4
p.m. on a Friday. Because of the threat of thunderstorms, my friend was
concerned. Before going to bed that evening, she lifted her family in
prayer. However, she was still nervous about their journey until she
received a text message around 9:45 p.m. from her daughter.

"Why am I so worried?" my friend asked herself.

Reassured by the text message, my friend went to sleep. Just as she dozed
off, however, her husband received a phone call, detailing car problems the
young couple had encountered in Texas. As my friend and her husband
communicated with their daughter, providing assistance via text messaging
and phone calls, her worry took over and my friend thought, "Now what?
Gotta do something else."

Over the next couple of hours, my friend and her husband tried to solve the
dilemma, looking up towing services and motels on the Internet and
forwarding the information to their daughter. In the meantime, her
daughter and family had made their own arrangements. Christina assured
her mother, "We're okay. Get some sleep. We'll talk in the morning."

Next morning's conversation between the two still revealed a mother's
worry. Even though the car had been repaired, my friend found herself
grilling her daughter. "Did he check the belts and the other hoses?"
Christina interrupted, telling her mother that everything was okay and they
were back on the road.

Thinking about this incident led my friend to open her Bible and read the
first chapter of James. Verses 23-25 say, "For if you listen to the word and
don't obey, it is like glancing at your face in a mirror. You see yourself,
walk away, and forget what you look like. But if you look carefully into

the perfect law that sets you free, and if you do what it says and don't forget what you heard, then God will bless you for doing it."

"It was describing me," says my friend. "I had looked in the mirror and saw God's promises. Then I turned away from that 'mirror of truth' and returned to my doubtful ways."

Why do we doubt God's promises when they are in black and white? Michael Angier, author of "Kicking the Worry Habit," says, "I came to the awareness that worry is like prayer in reverse."

Matthew 6:27 says, "Who of you by worrying can add a single hour to his life?" If it did, we'd never give up the habit.

Are you worrying your prayers?

What Are You Pursuing?

"And I saw that all labor and all achievement spring from man's envy of his neighbor. This too is meaningless, a chasing after the wind"
—Ecclesiastes 4:4(NIV).

A recent Saturday found a friend and me up early hitting garage sales to find bargains. I went along because she is new to the community and unfamiliar with the area. One garage sale sign led us to an upscale neighborhood where the owner also had his house on the market. As we browsed his treasures, I noticed several framed posters for sale, including one of a red Ferrari sports car. The message accompanying the photo was, "The one with the most toys wins."

The irony of that statement hit me, when through a conversation with the man running the garage sale, I deduced that he was going through or had gone through a divorce and was being forced to sell his house as well as many of the things he treasured. In spite of the obvious wealth he once must have had, he was selling material things or his toys, to strangers for a fraction of what they were worth.

My friend and I bought a few of the nice items he was offering because the prices were too good to pass up. However, the owner was intent on convincing us to buy more and touted the attributes of each thing he was parting with for a dollar or two. Most were priced under $20. After our few purchases, we headed to the car. Desperate to sell his treasures, the homeowner followed us. In spite of feeling sorry for him, I didn't buy anything else.

In the movie, "The Pursuit of Happyness," Chris Gardner, a struggling single parent who has lost his job, sees someone drive up to the curb in an expensive sports car. Gardner, played by Will Smith, asks, "Man, what do you do and how do you do it?" When the driver replies that he is a stockbroker, Gardner decides that he is going to pursue the same career. He wants to make a lot of money, buy a fancy car and live happily ever after.

While there is nothing wrong with owning nice things, if we replace the pursuit of them with the pursuit of a relationship with our Savior, we miss what is important in life. It's a chasing of the wind, as the writer of Ecclesiastes says, when we pursue wealth, yet are never satisfied with what we have.

When we drive a new automobile from the lot, it immediately begins to depreciate faster than the new car smell we covet. When we walk out of the store with the latest techie gadget, it's already on its way to becoming obsolete. This year's fashion is tomorrow's castoff.

Man was not created to pursue endlessly those things that only bring temporary satisfaction. Lasting contentment, peace and joy can only be found through something that money can never buy and no man can ever take away. They are gifts from our Heavenly Father and the only thing with enduring value.

Are you pursuing God's gifts?

Can You Fool God?

"There is nothing concealed that will not be disclosed, or hidden that will not be made known. What you have said in the dark will be heard in the daylight…" *–Luke 12:2-3(NIV)*.

"Have you ever tried to fool yourself?" That question would have haunted me in the past and it was one recently posed by our pastor during a Sunday morning sermon. We can all answer "Yes" to that question if we are being honest with ourselves.

I think it's much easier to fool others than it is to recognize that we are fooling ourselves when it comes to matters of the heart and of the spirit. Many of us wear masks, trying to hide our weaknesses and our fears. Others hide behind Christian symbols on their cars but don't recognize their own human frailties.

Using himself as an example, Pastor Ray shared this story. Returning from a hospital visit in a neighboring community, he was running late for a church appointment when he was caught in bottleneck traffic at an ongoing road construction site. As cars inched forward to merge into one lane, a vehicle sped by intent on getting as close to the front of the line as possible. Pastor Ray was indignant, especially when he saw the Christian fish symbol on the offender's automobile. Pastor Ray said he edged as close as possible to the vehicle in front of him to keep someone from squeezing in line in front of his truck.

However, when he noticed another car trying to merge unsuccessfully into the moving traffic lane, he was convicted by his own attitude. The driver, a woman, had a carload full of young children. If you have ever traveled with young children, you can probably relate to this woman's predicament.

How often though do we fool ourselves, thinking we are different from the rest of the world? As Pastor Ray said, "It is easy to see hypocrisy in others but difficult to see it in ourselves."

Before I rededicated my life to Jesus in 2001, I condemned those "hypocrites" in the church and used it as an excuse to drift away from my Christian roots. However, I also realize that I am no different. It's so easy to look inside the church walls while standing on the outside and find fault.

As Pastor Ray often reminds us, "The church is not a hotel for saints but a hospital for sinners." Romans 3:23 is a reminder that we have all sinned and fallen short of the glory of God.

Although we can fool ourselves, we can never fool God. We can't run away from Him and we can't hide. No matter where we turn, to the east or to the west, He is there. Even my six-year-old granddaughter knows that. Listening intently to one of Pastor Ray's sermons recently, she whispered to me, "Nana, you can't run away from God because He is always with you."

If a child can proclaim the truth, why can't we recognize it?

Which One Will You Feed?

"Trust in the Lord always, for the Lord God is the eternal Rock"
–Isaiah 26:4 (NLT).

Would people say you are a peaceful person? According to the Online Etymology Dictionary, the meaning, from the mid-14th century, comes from two words "peace" + "ful," and means tranquil and calm. Now, ask yourself, am I full of peace?

If you don't have peace, would you say you are broken, anxious, troubled, depressed, frustrated, exhausted or worried? Maybe you are all of these. Did you know if you are continually without peace, it could lead to health problems?

According to the Mayo Clinic, 80 to 85% of their caseloads can be attributed to stress. In addition, an article in a leading medical journal questioned, "Is Stress the Cause of all Disease?" According to the study, bacteria were the leading cause of illness at the beginning of the century. However, stress has surpassed bacteria as the number one reason of health-related problems today.

Did you know that one of the antonyms, or an opposite of the word "stress," is peace? However, you can't pursue peace or run away from stress. Some people try to escape through alcohol, drugs, food and the wrong relationships. Some of us become workaholics while others choose to procrastinate.

When we learn that peace is not a place, a thing or a destination but a journey, we will find that inner calm, even in the valleys of life. Peace is not the absence of problems or trials. The peace that passes understanding is having a calm confidence that our God is bigger than any problem we face in life. No valley is too deep for Him to lead us out.

I have to remember the following when I am tempted to let life's trials rob me of my peace: *"God, grant me the serenity to accept the things I cannot change, Courage to change the things I can, and the Wisdom to know the difference."*

I also like this reminder, an acronym, PUSH. Pray Until Something Happens. Our lives are full of people and concerns that we need to turn over to God in prayer. Philippians 4:6 says, "Do not be anxious about anything, but in everything, by prayer and petition, with thanksgiving, present your requests to God."

If we trust God to supply all our needs, then why do we continue to worry and let it rob us of our peace? We have two alternatives in life when it comes to our trials. We can pray, trusting that our Heavenly Father has a better plan than we could ever imagine, or we can fret about it until we are robbed of that inner calm promised to us by our Savior. Just like Peter, who took his eyes off Jesus, we can sink into despair if we don't keep walking toward Him.

We all have plenty of fodder for prayer material. Another word for fodder is feed. Therefore, we can feed our prayers and trust God to provide an answer or we can feed our worries.

Which one will you feed?

But God, it Hurts So Much

"Consider it pure joy, my brothers, whenever you face trials of many kinds, because you know that the testing of your faith develops perseverance. Perseverance must finish its work so that you may be mature and complete, not lacking anything"—James 1:2-3 (NIV).

As a child, I can remember my mother giving me leg rubs at bedtime, not every night, but when my legs ached from playing too hard. However, she used to tell me I was having growing pains. I never thought much about my mother's diagnosis until my granddaughter started complaining with leg pains after going to bed.

Recently, I read that about 25 to 40 percent of children will experience growing pains, a normal occurrence, generally striking during two periods: in early childhood among 3- to 5-year-olds and, later, in 8- to 12-year-olds. However, there is no firm evidence that the growth of bones causes pain. The most likely causes of aches and discomforts result from the jumping, climbing and running that active kids do while playing during the day. Doctors say that the pains are always concentrated in the muscles, rather than the joints with most kids reporting pain in the front of their thighs, in the calves or behind the knees.

No one really likes to experience pain of any kind but in James 1:2-3, he tells us as Christians to count it as pure joy when we face trials. Pure joy? Yes, pure joy because our growing pains will help us to grow up in Christ. Notice that James doesn't say, "If we face trials," but "when we face trials of many kinds."

Although that sounds daunting, James' advice is encouraging. Why? Because "God is our refuge and strength, an ever-present help in trouble."

As an adult, I have questioned God about my "growing pains." Sometimes, it seems never-ending. Other times, He allows me to experience a brief victory on the mountaintop. I don't think He wants me to get too comfortable up on that mountain. About the time I think I have arrived, life gives me more lemons. I just get tired of squeezing them sometimes. I can only drink so much lemonade.

Sometimes the pain of spiritual growth has been so intense that I have called out to God, asking Him why I have to go through it. I know I don't want to go around it like the Israelites who kept going around the same mountain for 40 years. However, if trials build character, then I ought to have the best. Evidently, God doesn't think so.

While I have mastered making lemonade, there are other fruits, like those of the Spirit that still need developing. I am so imperfect yet He hasn't given up on me. He is still molding me and shaping me to be more like Jesus.

God doesn't give up on those who truly seek to be changed. If you are on a pilgrimage, your journey, like mine, won't end until we cross over to heaven's side and our Savior says, "Well done, my good and faithful servant."

I anticipate hearing those words someday. Do you?

Where are Your Bruises?

"The Lord is close to the brokenhearted
and saves those who are crushed in spirit"—Psalm 34:18 (NIV).

In my lifetime, I've fallen while roller skating, banged my shin on the coffee table, and run into a wall and awakened with a wallop of a bruise more times than I can count. I hate to admit I'm not the most coordinated person and I'm always surprised when I find another bruise I cannot explain. It's also why I seldom wear high heels.

Recently, I purchased a new bicycle as a challenge to my workout routine. I'm not accustomed to one that has more gears than my 2001 Honda Passport but I'm learning. The owner's manual for my bike is almost 50 pages long, while the cover proclaims it is Version 9.0. I thought only software upgrades carried that warning, meaning it is more complicated than the previous one. The table of contents reads like a Pentagon's strategic plan for action with step-by-step guidelines that include everything from your first ride to service intervals and what to do if your bicycle sustains an impact. I immediately went to page 32 of the manual to read about the latter. I knew I needed to be prepared.

At the time of my purchase, I browsed the store, which carried a variety of accessories for two-wheeled fun. I settled on an approved safety helmet and thought about how bicycles had changed since I was a kid. Bike helmets didn't exist and we certainly didn't have a 50-page instruction book. After graduating from training wheels, riding a bike was as simple as climbing on and pedaling.

If only life were as simple as climbing on a bicycle and pedaling. After passing certain tests and leaving our training wheels behind, shouldn't life be easier? It's not. We live in a bruised and broken world. We make wrong choices and we get off God's perfect path. We get hurt, we suffer disappointments and sometimes we think the pain will never go away. And even though we may not sport physical bruises, the emotional wounds run deep.

However, there is a cure for a bruised soul. Our God has a soft spot for those who are suffering. The psalmist said, "The Lord is close to the brokenhearted, and saves those who are crushed in spirit." Psalm 147:3 reads, "He heals the brokenhearted and binds up their wounds."

In 2 Corinthians, Paul writes about the thorn in his side. He pleads three times for the Lord to take it away. But Christ says, "My grace is sufficient for you, for my power is made perfect in weakness." Paul continues in the same passage, saying, "For when I am weak, then I am strong."

If our sufferings bring us closer to God and we become stronger, should we then consider our wounds as blessings? Jesus said, "Blessed are the poor in spirit, for theirs is the kingdom of heaven."

Where are your bruises? Consider yourself blessed if they draw you closer to our Abba Father. That's when the healing begins.

If God had a Facebook Page

"My heart says of you, 'Seek his face!'
Your face, Lord, I will seek"—*Psalm 17:8 (NIV).*

When I finally decided to join Facebook, five years after it was launched, I was excited when I reconnected with many of my former students and teaching peers. After a 30-year career on the high school level, I was not always able to keep track of where life had led many of them, especially the quieter ones.

Not too long after I signed up on Facebook, I received an email from a young man who had graduated in 1978. Cecil wasn't sure if I remembered him. I did. When I accepted his friend request, I learned that he had spent many years fighting alcohol and drug addiction. However, his message said, "God has seen fit to give me another chance."

Cecil is now the ministry leader for Celebrate Recovery at a church in northeastern Oklahoma. I was not only touched that he had shared his story, but the following words made me realize how we all have a positive role to play in each other's lives: "You don't know it, but you played a big part in my pulling through. I remember you always encouraged me and lifted me up. Thanks."

While we may never know the impact our positive words and actions have on someone else, I was blessed, through a social networking site, to know that I had made a difference in Cecil's life.

At first, I was reluctant to embrace this website until I was encouraged by friends who use it for business purposes. As a writer, I thought it would be a great opportunity for me to connect with likeminded people. I wasn't prepared, however, for the explosion of re-connections I have made with former classmates and students, like Cecil. Most recently, I have reconnected with childhood friends in Louisiana. We have been tripping down nostalgia lane as we have corresponded about our favorite memories and caught up with each other's life events of the past 40 years.

When Mark Zuckerberg started Facebook for his classmates, I am sure he did not anticipate the revolution it would bring to our world. In a recent newspaper article about the growth of the company, some of Zuckerberg's employees candidly used the word "ubiquity" to describe the company's goal to the reporter.

Look up the word "ubiquity" in the dictionary and this is what you will find: "the state or capacity of being everywhere, especially at the same time; omnipresence; in theology, the omnipresence of God or Christ." Originally, the word was a Lutheran theological position maintaining the omnipresence of Christ.

If God had a Facebook page, would you seek His friendship? Would you communicate with Him each day? I know He would seek your friendship. He wants a personal relationship with each one of His children. We can be confident that when we seek His face, He is always there. Furthermore, we don't need a social networking site to connect.

As the psalmist says, "Your face, Lord, will I seek."

Is Your Light Shining?

"He is like a tree planted by streams of water, which yields its fruit in season and whose leaf does not wither. Whatever he does prospers"
—*Psalm 1:3 (NIV).*

As a new season is underway, I marvel at the beauty of nature with the changing colors of the trees. Even as a child in Louisiana, I loved what nature had to offer, although the seasons were not as distinct. On a recent return to the state of my birth, I enjoyed a boat ride down the Bayou Teche through a maze of beauty with its bald cypress trees and 100-year-old live oaks draped in Spanish moss.

The bald cypress trees appear to emerge from the water. With age, the dramatic looking tree forms "knees" that grow up from the roots for stability. These monarchs of the swamp thrive in the alluvial soil deposited by the flowing water of the bayou, and can grow as high as 100 feet and up to 15 feet in diameter over hundreds of years.

As our guide boat wended its way through the bayou on that sunny September afternoon, I recalled my childhood trips down the same waterways with my father at the helm. My sister and I enjoyed the intrigue and mystery of the land with its varied wildlife, including alligators, ibises, egrets, herons, water moccasins and cottonmouths. However, seeing the lush green tropical growth and God's creatures through adult eyes gave me a new respect for the seasons of my own life.

I was in my late 40s when I began to ask the question, "Who am I?" This led me on a search for the girl who had grown up in that Louisiana paradise. During this time of reflection, I found myself attracted to paintings and photographs of magnolia trees and their creamy white flowers, another childhood memory. Even though magnolia trees are slow growing, I planted one in my front yard last spring. More recently, I dug a hole for a weeping willow, another favorite from my youth. The weeping willow is, however, a fast growing tree.

Any tree, when planted, must have a good foundation with the correct soil and plenty of water until its root system is established; otherwise, it won't survive. The same is true of our Christian walk. Once we accept God's gift of grace, our transformation begins. In addition, when we allow Him fully into our lives, a radical change occurs. As we let go of our past and accept our new life in Him, we begin to bear fruit.

A recent email I received compared being a Christian to being a pumpkin. "God lifts you up, takes you in and washes all the dirt off you. He opens you up, touches you deep inside and scoops out all the yucky stuff, including the seeds of doubt, hate and greed. Then, He carves you a new smiling face and puts His light inside you to shine for the entire world to see."

I love that comparison. Is your light shining for the entire world to see?

Alligators, Ants and Snakes, Oh my!

"For God has not given us a spirit of fear and timidity, but of power, love, and self-discipline"—*2 Timothy 1:7 (NLT)*.

As a child, I was afraid of many things. However, the fear that tormented my child's mind the most occurred in the darkness after my mother turned out the bedroom light. I was afraid of the shadows cast by the unknown and reflected in the tiny night light she left burning to allay my fears.

As I grew, my fears were related to relationships and social activities. Being chosen last in elementary school when we split up for games at recess or during physical education classes led me to dread those times. I was not athletically inclined; however, I discovered in my mid-40s that I could compete and win in 5K races. Although I entered my first race for fun, once I discovered that I could run the 3.1 miles, I was hooked. At first, I was competing against others. Later, it became a matter of improving my own time, whether I won or not. While I still have the trophies and medals I won in those races, I have learned lessons more important than these outward signs of victory—lessons of eternal value.

In a recent sermon series titled, "The Journey Home," our pastor used the characters from "The Wizard of Oz" to address our human condition and a need for God to fill that emptiness in our hearts that nothing else can. In this memorable movie, Dorothy is trying to find her way back to Kansas where she lives on a farm with her family. Along the yellow brick road, she meets various characters, including the cowardly lion. If you've seen the movie, you know he was afraid of everything, including Dorothy's dog, Toto.

2 Timothy 1:7 says, "For God has not given us a spirit of fear and timidity, but of power, love and self-discipline." Many people fear the unknown, including what others think about them. In the past, that was me. Once I began to live for God, I cast off the fear of rejection and learned to step out in faith. Ancient Greeks believed that courage is the foundation of all virtues. It takes courage to leave our past behind. It takes faith to believe Jesus wants what is best for us, and courage to step out and follow Him.

Since moving to a new community almost seven years ago, my faith has led me on three mission trips, including one inside the U.S. border. Before departing and upon arrival, we received cautionary warnings about certain dangers, including the alligators, fire ants and snakes that inhabit the swampy areas of Louisiana.

While it is wise to be cautious, when we embrace the unknown without fear, God is with us and we are safe in His care. What is the spirit of fear preventing you from accomplishing?

If you had the courage, what would you do for God?

Seeing the Living Hope

"Though you have not seen Him, you love Him; and even though you do not see Him now, you believe in Him and are filled with an inexpressible and glorious joy"—*1 Peter1:8 (NIV)*.

Cleaning out my vehicle recently, I found a large withered leaf in the floorboard. The reddish-brown foliage crumbled in my hands when I picked it up. It was a reminder of my granddaughter's love.

Several days earlier, I had visited my grandchildren at school. After lunch, we went to the playground where I played with them as well as several of their friends. Cheyenne and her playmates began gathering red, yellow, brown, gold and other autumn-colored leaves from the ground. My granddaughter was enthralled with the variety of colors, shapes and sizes as well as the detail of each leaf, which she pointed out to me before placing them in my hands to hold.

Her classmates began to do the same and both my hands soon overflowed with evidence of the new season. Rising from the bench where I had been sitting, I asked the small crowd, "Do you want to be leafed?" All yelled, "Yes," in unison but then wanted to know what I meant. I explained that I was going to toss the handfuls of leaves in the air to rain down on them. Excited, they spread out, laughing as the confetti of colorful foliage floated through the breeze. Of course, once was not enough and I continued the game, until the teacher's whistle announced recess was over. Before Cheyenne ran to line up, she gave me one of the rust-colored leaves, the one I discovered several days later in my car.

Because the leaf had dried out, I tossed it into the trash and remembered the youthful enthusiasm of the children. Later that day, while walking through a nearby field, I paid more attention to the variety of leaves scattered on the ground. Picking several up, I examined them carefully, just as my granddaughter had done. The scattered foliage reminded me of our lives. With each season, we experience different stages of change. How we deal with these differences defines our lives.

The apostle Peter, offering encouragement to persecuted Christians scattered throughout Asia Minor, says, "Though you have not seen Him, you love Him; and even though you do not see Him now, you believe in Him and are filled with an inexpressible and glorious joy."

The joy I saw that day in the faces of the children as they chased the breeze-blown leaves reminded me that each season of our lives, no matter how difficult, is a time for believing and hoping. Faith brings the promise of another day and a new season, even when we can't see it.

We all face trials in our lives. Whether it is a job loss, the loss of a loved one, the loss of our home or the loss of a relationship, we can rest assured that even though we cannot see Him now, if we believe in Him, we will be filled with a living Hope.

Who Is Watching You?

"Therefore be imitators of God as dear children"—*Ephesians 5:1 (NKJV)*.

Whether you are a parent, or now a grandparent, seeing young children through His eyes can bring new meaning to life. My youngest grandson, who just celebrated his first birthday in September, wore a cow costume to our Fall Festival at church. I don't think I've ever seen a cuter cow but then, I am his grandmother.

Children at the festival celebration enjoyed a variety of activities, designed for fun and fellowship, including a Cake Walk. Before the music started playing, 10 participants stood in a circle, their feet firmly planted on a cardboard circle with an assigned number. When the music started, feet began moving from one circle to the next. When the music stopped, a number was announced and the winner could pick out his favorite cake or cupcake as a prize.

Although my grandson and I participated in the Cake Walk, we didn't win a prize. It didn't matter, however, because watching Cash dance to the music filled this grandmother's heart with joy. Later that day, I recalled his smiling face peeking out from the costume while he danced to the sound of a contemporary Christian song, and I thought about small children imitating others.

Children emulate the actions and words of others. That is how they learn. Speech is learned by mimicking sounds and then connecting them to objects, people or ideas. As parents and grandparents, we get excited when we hear a child's first word. We watch toddlers reenact events by watching others. Sometimes it is humorous; other times it can be uncomfortable.

Just as children learn by imitating adults, God's children learn by imitating Him. If you look up the definition of "imitator," the first entry reads, "to follow or endeavor to follow as a model or example." More than one scripture encourages us to be imitators of our Savior. Ephesians 5:1 tells us to be "imitators of God as dear children." Can you imagine the joy in our Heavenly Father's heart when He sees His children imitating His Son?

To be a child of God means striving everyday to follow His word and live out His commands. It isn't easy because we are constantly bombarded with worldly messages. Rock stars, movie stars and others in the limelight become heroes to some and many would rather emulate their lifestyles than that of a humble carpenter who came to save us from ourselves.

In 1 Corinthians 11:1, the apostle Paul encourages us to follow his example, "as I follow the example of Christ." Paul exemplified a true imitator of Christ. As Paul learned, however, following Christ is not easy. No one ever promised it would be an easy task for any of us. However, trusting in the Lord, and following His lead, helps us to understand that all things will be used for His purposes. If we imitate the greatest Teacher, can we ever go wrong?

Are you an imitator of Christ? What type of example do you set?

What is Your Response?

"Give thanks to the Lord, for he is good; his love endures forever"
—1 Chronicles 16:34 (NIV).

After listening to more than one sermon and reading more than one devotional about being thankful, I have consciously adopted an attitude of gratitude. Sometimes, it's not easy in a world filled with so much negativity, especially during an election year. With daily headlines and news bites focusing on the gloomy economy and unexpected disasters, it's sometimes hard to stay focused on the positive.

Recently, I changed my vocabulary to reflect my choice to be more confident. Remember David's response in Psalm 27:13? "I remain confident of this: I will see the goodness of the Lord in the land of the living."

One way I am remaining confident is in my response to the question, "How are you today?" In the past, I might have complained about fluctuating gas prices, traffic jams and rude drivers as well as the price of tea in China. It only made me feel more miserable and I am sure that my questioner was left even more depressed by my response. Now, I put a smile on my face and reply, "I am doing wonderful. How about you?"

Recently, while checking out at a local convenience store, the clerk asked, "How are you today?" I responded with my new attitude and he replied, "I'm doing great!"

Our conversation continued when I said, "You know what, it doesn't do any good to complain. It's not going to change anything. Although it might give us a temporary high to focus on the negative, it only leaves us more depressed."

The clerk replied, "If more people felt that way, our world would be a better place." Later that day, I reflected on this young man's response and recalled the people I have met while traveling to other countries for mission trips and on spiritual pilgrimages. Even in the midst of poverty, I have witnessed smiles of gratitude and hope.

Our 16th president, Abraham Lincoln, said, "Most folks are about as happy as they make their minds up to be." Happiness, according to the dictionary, is based on luck or good fortune while joy is described as a state of well-being and contentment. Happiness, then, depends on our circumstances while joy is our emotional well-being. When we recognize that joy does not depend on winning the lottery, getting a bigger car or living in a McMansion, then we begin to recognize the strength of this emotion as part of our daily lives, a part of who we are and how we view the world.

Try this. Make a list of what you have to be thankful for and share it with others, including God. My gratitude list is long but here are a few: a loving family, precious friends, my church family, good health, a part-time job, a reliable vehicle, a roof over my head, living in a country where I can express my faith and not be persecuted. But, most of all, I give thanks to God, for He is my salvation.

What is on your thanks-giving list?

Sharing Your Blessings

"The generous will themselves be blessed, for they share their food with the poor" —*Proverbs 22:9 (NIV).*

Positive news from the media always attracts my attention in this negative, broken world. It's especially uplifting to hear of the good deeds of others, even when that individual is in the midst of disappointment or pain. Recently, a news report revealed the story of a young woman in Colorado Springs whose wedding ceremony was called off two days before the planned event. Instead of focusing on herself, the young woman decided to use the occasion to bless others.

The bride-to-be's parents had planned a lavish Saturday night feast after the ceremony. Instead of letting the food go to waste, the young woman told her parents that she wanted to feed the less fortunate, many of whom are homeless. With the help of the Salvation Army, the family used this opportunity to reach out to others and surprise them with an early Thanksgiving dinner. A Salvation Army representative said that the hot meal on a very cold night also warmed many hearts. "In all my years, I have never seen anything like this," he said.

Although the young woman was not interviewed on camera, the father had this to say about his daughter. "She is a super giving young lady," he said. "I have been blessed with two wonderful daughters and was not surprised when she chose to do this."

We make choices each day, some good and some not so good. However, every decision we make has consequences. One choice that will radically change your life and those around you is the one that recognizes the world does not revolve around you. We are here for a purpose and the greatest joy in life comes when we are set free to meet the needs of others.

Recently, I was visiting with a new friend about his travels to the Ukraine in the former USSR. As Brian described his travels and the people he had met, he said, "After visiting the Ukraine, I realized I was more materialistic than I thought."

Commenting on the smiles he saw on the faces of the Ukrainians, Brian said, "I wondered how they could be so happy when they had so little." Having traveled to Mexico on a mission trip several years ago, I could relate to Brian's statement. Even in the midst of poverty, I saw contentment through the smiles of the poorest.

I saw those same radiant smiles on the faces of those who lived in the most poverty-stricken areas of Israel last spring. Even in their lack, they appeared richer than many in our country where our wants have become necessities.

As we start this holiday season, let's remember to give thanks by sharing with others who are less fortunate and begin Advent celebrating our values and not focusing on material things. The rush to grab our hard-earned dollars started earlier than usual this year. While there is nothing wrong with buying presents and getting a bargain, don't forget others who have so much less than you.

How can you share your blessings with others?

One Size Does Fit All

"Peace I leave with you; my peace I give you. I do not give to you as the world gives. Do not let your hearts be troubled and do not be afraid"
—*John 14:27 (NIV).*

Have you ever purchased a "one-size-fits-all" piece of clothing, only to find it wasn't true? Maybe the sleeves were a little too long or the shoulder seams drooped almost to your elbows. Maybe you bought it for someone else as a gift but it just didn't fit. Or maybe you struggle with finding the right present at this time of year for someone and opt for a gift card or cash instead.

However, one Christmas gift fits everyone. Size is not a concern. It doesn't need batteries or any other accessories. You don't have to stay up late on Christmas Eve to assemble it. Wrapping paper and bows are unnecessary. Before I reveal this "one size fits all" gift, I want to share a story. I didn't realize the impact my words of encouragement had made on an older woman at church until she thanked me, once again, for a present I had given her several years ago. The priceless gift was not tangible, meaning she couldn't hold it in her hands but she still held it in her heart.

While interviewing this woman for a magazine article, I learned Audrey's secret. Hoping to help others by sharing her story, Audrey confessed that she had carried around guilt for 30 years. The burden she still shouldered involved an issue with a grown daughter and a stillborn grandchild. During our conversation, I felt lead to help this woman reconcile her past. I don't take credit for what happened during the course of the interview. I knew God was in the moment, giving me the words that this precious grandmother needed to hear for healing.

Audrey and I were visiting at church recently. When she hugged me and asked how I was doing, I replied, "I am filled with more peace than I have been in a long time."

With that comment, Audrey replied, "And I am too, thanks to you." After releasing her burdens to the Lord and taking steps to rectify her past, she discovered the peace that passes all understanding. Peace is the gift that keeps on giving.

As Christmas nears, let us remember that Jesus is the Prince of Peace. Peace came wrapped, not in a bright shiny package, but in swaddling clothes. Christmas is a powerful reminder that Christ came to redeem us.

Christ came so that we might have peace with God, peace with ourselves and peace with others. Do you remember the words to the song, "Let there be peace on earth?" Part of the lyrics are "Let there be peace on earth and let it begin with me."

Peace is the perfect one-size-fits-all gift. Where can you find it? It's simple and it doesn't cost a dime. Just welcome the Prince of Peace into your heart and ask Him to take your burdens and guilt.

And don't forget to offer forgiveness to those who have wronged you.

In a Field Nearby

"...and there were shepherds living out in the fields nearby, keeping watch over their flocks at night. An angel of the Lord appeared to them, and the glory of the Lord shone around them, and they were terrified. But the angel said to them, 'Do not be afraid. I bring you good news that will cause great joy for all the people. Today in the town of David a Savior has been born to you; he is the Messiah, the Lord. This will be a sign to you: You will find a baby wrapped in cloths and lying in a manger'"

—Luke 2:8-12 (NIV).

Inhaling the fresh air, I closed my eyes to picture the scene on that night over 2,000 years ago. On a spiritual pilgrimage with other church members, I stood in a spot overlooking the fields just east of Bethlehem identified since ancient times with the shepherds who were the first to hear the Good News.

Although it has been more than two years since our Holy Land tour, I can still recall the night we visited the Shepherd's Fields, where we closed our eyes and imagined what the shepherds would have been doing on the night when the angel of the Lord appeared. They might have been talking quietly in the blackness of the cold, winter sky before the hillside was suddenly ablaze with light and the booming sound of an angel's voice. Luke 2:9 says, "An angel of the Lord appeared to them, and the glory of the Lord shone around them, and they were terrified."

Can you imagine their terror? I can. I have also wondered why shepherds were the first ones told of the birth of Christ. According to "Unger's Bible Dictionary," shepherds lived a life of hardship and even danger. Not only were they exposed to the extremes of heat and cold, their food frequently consisted of what they could forage. Wild animals and the possibility of robbery were also constant threats.

For protection, a shepherd would have with him a mantle or cloak, probably made of sheepskin, for warmth. He also carried a scrip or wallet, containing a small amount of food. In addition to a sling as a weapon, he also carried a staff. It served the dual purpose of a weapon against foes and a crook for the management of the flock.

Shepherds held down jobs that were one of the least desirable in ancient times. The hours were long, the pay was low and their social status was certainly not at the top of the ladder. Maybe their skills were limited and they had trouble finding work elsewhere. I am certain, however, that they were not expecting a heavenly visit while on watch. Why would God send such an important message to these shepherds instead of high officials? Why were the shepherds tending their flocks the first to know?

Jesus came to change and save the world, including those who were the least among men.

Isn't that the greatest news of all?

Just For Today

"This is the day the Lord has made.
We will rejoice and be glad in it"—*Psalm 118:24 (NLT).*

Did you know that 97 percent of New Year's resolutions are never fulfilled? Oscar Wilde wrote, "A New Year's resolution is something that goes in one year and out the other."

Although 45 percent of us make New Year's resolutions, many eventually ditch them, with 75 percent making it past the first week and 46 percent making it past the six-month mark.

According to research, most fail at following through because of unrealistic expectations, like "I'm going to lose 30 pounds by February 1." While there is nothing wrong with making resolutions, when we set the bar too high, we are setting ourselves up for failure. What if we decided, just for today, we would do one thing to improve our physical, emotional or, more importantly, our spiritual health?

Author Jim Liebelt offers the following suggestions in hopes we might incorporate some into our daily lives.

- Just for today, resolve to pray.
- Just for today, resolve to say, "I love you" to someone.
- Just for today, resolve to appreciate the world around you.
- Just for today, resolve to save money.
- Just for today, resolve to forgive someone.
- Just for today, resolve not to compare yourself to anyone else.
- Just for today, resolve to create some warmth in your home.
- Just for today, resolve to exercise.
- Just for today, resolve to read from the Bible.
- Just for today, resolve to eat less.
- Just for today, resolve to prepare for a future event.
- Just for today, resolve not to demand the last word.
- Just for today, resolve to make the most of that day.
- Just for today, resolve to learn something new.
- Just for today, resolve to eat a food you enjoy.
- Just for today, resolve to say, "Please."
- Just for today, resolve to laugh.

- Just for today, resolve to do something unusually nice for a family member.
- Just for today, resolve to forgive yourself.
- Just for today resolve to sleep in.
- Just for today, resolve to spend some time with family.
- Just for today, resolve to be kind.
- Just for today, resolve to give someone a choice.
- Just for today, resolve to make someone laugh.
- Just for today, resolve to do something nice for someone outside of your family.
- Just for today, resolve to say, "thank you."
- Just for today, resolve to pay someone a compliment.
- Just for today, resolve to do something relaxing.
- Just for today, resolve to do something nice for a complete stranger.
- Just for today, resolve to do something out of the ordinary.

I would also add—just for today—let us rejoice and be glad in the day the Lord has made.

Has Your Identity Been Stolen?

"This means that anyone who belongs to Christ has become a new person. The old life is gone; a new life has begun"—*2 Corinthians 5:17(NLT).*

Identify theft, according to Javelin Strategy & Research, decreased in 2010. However, according to their website, consumer costs, the average out-of-pocket dollar amount victims pay, increased, reversing a downward trend in recent years. With 11.1 million adults becoming victims of identity theft, billions of dollars are lost to frauds.

ID theft occurs when an impostor obtains key pieces of personal information such as Social Security numbers and driver's license numbers and uses them for their own personal gain. Lost or stolen wallets, pilfered mail, a data breach, computer virus, phishing, fraud or paper documents thrown out by an individual or a business can be the start of ID theft. Although the crime varies widely, it can include check fraud, credit card fraud, financial identity theft, criminal identity theft, governmental identity theft and identity fraud.

According to the Identity Theft Resource Center (ITRC), a nonprofit organization dedicated exclusively to the understanding and prevention of identity theft, victims experience a wide range of emotions, including at times, feeling overwhelmed by the psychological pain of loss, helplessness, anger, isolation, betrayal, rage and even embarrassment. Victims of this crime can also experience the inability to ever trust again.

Another type of identity theft has also become epidemic in our country. This theft is not as obvious but its effects are just as emotional and one to which many of us can relate. This theft robs us of our identity in Christ. If we do not know who we are in Christ, then peer pressure can lead us to be something we are not. God did not create us to be someone else.

Did you know that with the increase in ID theft, companies are now offering insurance to protect people from becoming victims? Did you know that God has a better insurance plan?

In Ephesians 1: 4-5, Paul writes, "For he chose us in him before the creation of the world to be holy and blameless in his sight. In love, he predestined us for adoption to sonship through Jesus Christ, in accordance with his pleasure and will to the praise of his glorious grace, which he has freely given us in the One he loves."

For most of my life, I didn't know who I was in Christ. I became a people pleaser because I was insecure in my own skin. For years, I allowed others to rob me of my identity. Ten years ago, events led me to my knees where my journey as a new person began. It was out with the old and in with the new. Just as we celebrate a new year, we can celebrate when we allow God to reshape our identity in Christ.

If your spiritual identity has been stolen, there is a simple solution. When you accept Jesus Christ as your Lord and Savior, you are made new.

And that's the best insurance of all.

Is Your Faith Waxing or Waning?

"Faith is being sure of what we hope for. It is being certain of what we do not see"—Hebrews 11:1 (NIRV).

Raise your hand if you've ever doubted God. If you're a believer, like me, I bet you have too. Why? Because, in our humanness, we sometimes forget that we are not really in control of the universe. We forget that God has a better plan.

Since signing up for a Facebook account almost two years ago, I have been delighted to reconnect with those whose lives no longer cross my path except for online. Recently, a former student posted the following quote: "God most definitely will give us more than we can handle. How else will we learn to rely on God in faith?"

Although I asked, Haley didn't know the source of this quote. However, it made me think. I can recall a glib response I've heard, and even made to people who were struggling. That popular response is "God never gives us more than we can handle."

Now, if that were true, then we would never have the need to go to Him with our burdens. In Matthew 11:28, Jesus says, "Come to me, all you who are weary and burdened, and I will give you rest."

My trials have increased since I reached out for my Savior in the fall of 2001. Since that day, my faith has grown as He has shown me His faithfulness. However, I have learned that faith makes things possible, not easier. And, I often wonder about those who struggle through life without knowing and trusting God.

Our faith is unique, in that it can grow stronger, even in the face of hardship and sorrow. However, if we neglect to nourish it, it can wane. If we compare our faith to the month-long lunar day, we can see the different phases of the moon and its appearance to us. When the moon is new and before it reaches half-lit, it's getting bigger and is still shaped like a crescent. It is waxing. After the half-illumination point, it is considered to be waning, or getting smaller.

Therefore, if we want our faith to grow, we have to nourish it so it will wax and not wane. What is the best way to increase our faith? First, we have to make prayer a daily habit. Putting God first at the beginning of each day by reading scripture and talking to God gives us the fodder we need for our faith to grow. I have also added prayer journaling to my list of spiritual disciplines. Seeing my words inked on the lined page has given me courage to become more authentic with my Abba Father.

In 1 Peter 1:6-7, the apostle writes, "In all this you greatly rejoice, though now for a little while you may have had to suffer grief in all kinds of trials. These have come so that the proven genuineness of your faith—of greater worth than gold, which perishes even though refined by fire—may result in praise, glory and honor when Jesus Christ is revealed."

Without trials and without grief, we cannot grow. They teach us to rely on God in faith.

Is your faith waxing or waning?

Are You Disconnected from God?

"No, the message isn't far away at all. In fact, it's really near you. It's in your mouth and in your heart so that you can obey it. Today I'm giving you a choice. You can have life and success. Or you can have death and harm"—*Deuteronomy 30:14-15 (NIRV)*.

If someone asked you about your connection to God, how would you answer? You might look at them strangely and ask, "What do you mean?" You might also reply, "Well, I go to church every Sunday. I pray and I read my Bible every day, or almost every day. Doesn't that count?"

Attending church on a regular basis, daily prayer and reading the Bible are ways to connect with God. However, a statement made by a medical expert on television recently made me think about connections that actually keep us from a deeper relationship with our Heavenly Father. The show's theme for the day was "20 Must-Do Things to Jumpstart Your Day."

The focus was on those things that keep us from getting out of bed in the morning refreshed and ready for the new day. The segment also included hints for people who are night owls yet have to rise early for work the next day or for those who have trouble sleeping for a variety of reasons, including food choices, room temperature and distractions like television and other electronic devices.

When one doctor revealed he knew of individuals who sleep with their cell phones, I could relate. I don't sleep with mine but I know people who do, people who are afraid of being disconnected from the world and the constant updates from friends and news sources. While there is nothing wrong with staying in touch with friends or keeping up with the news, it can lead us to disconnect from the most important relationship of all.

According to "dictionary.com," the following are synonyms for the word disconnect: break it off, break it up, cut off, detach, disassociate, disengage, disjoin, disunite, divide, drop it, part, separate and sever. We can allow our need to stay connected to the world 24/7 via electronic devices to separate us from God if we don't turn them off or lay them down to communicate with Him each day.

I confess that I panic when I can't locate my cell phone. Well, maybe panic is too strong a word, but I do get frustrated when I misplace it. That is why I keep a home phone. I can use it to call my cell when it comes up missing.

However, I never panic about losing God. He is always waiting patiently for each of us to disconnect from the cacophony of everyday life and spend quiet time with Him. In Psalm 46:10, He says, "Be still, and know that I am God; I will be exalted among the nations, I will be exalted in the earth."

Are you connected to God or have you let worldly distractions keep you from knowing Him?

How Do You Love?

"Dear children, let us not love with words or tongue but with actions and in truth"—*1 John 3:18 (NIV)*.

On a blue-lined piece of paper torn from a spiral notebook, my granddaughter created her version of a Valentine card for me. I've had it hanging on my refrigerator since she wrote the following words inside a heart shape, "I Love You Nana. Love Chey. You Rock." However, this sentiment was given to me several months ago, the day after Thanksgiving.

On February 14, we recognize those we love. While the card stores, flower shops, candy makers and other retailers also benefit on this annual holiday, we sometimes forget that love should be demonstrated every day. This doesn't mean you have to buy a dozen red roses or a calorie-laden box of chocolates daily to show your love to someone.

Just what is love? We all have pre-conceived notions of what that word means. For a starry-eyed teen or a single person looking for love in all the wrong places, the word romance comes to mind. However, that's not the definition Jesus had in mind when He said, "You shall love the Lord your God with all your heart, with all your soul, and with all your mind. This is the first and greatest commandment. And the second is like it: You shall love your neighbor as yourself. On these two commandments hang all the Law and the Prophets."

In an e-mail circulated for many years, a group of professionals posed this question to a group of youngsters: "What does love mean?" I like to revisit their definitions because they are a wonderful reminder of Christ's answer.

Rebecca, age 8, said, "When my grandmother got arthritis, she couldn't bend over and paint her toenails anymore. So my grandfather does it for her all the time, even when his hands got arthritis too. That's love."

Seven-year-old Danny explains love this way. "Love is when my mommy makes coffee for my daddy and she takes a sip before giving it to him, to make sure the taste is okay."

Nikka, age 6, really has a grasp of what it truly means to love. She said, "If you want to learn to love better, you should start with a friend whom you hate." Isn't that what Jesus said?

Did you know that love is a choice? Although our emotions are involved, they cannot be our only criteria for love. When we love as God loves us, unconditionally and unselfishly, we understand love in action. He loved us so much that He gave His only begotten Son that we might have life and love everlasting.

Do you know what happens when we pass on the love we have received from Him, love that we don't even deserve? When we let love flow through us, it multiplies beyond measure. When we love in deed and in truth, it comes back to us. We have God's promise that what we give will be given back many times over.

Isn't that the real currency of love?

How Tall Are Your Boots?

"Praise be to the Lord, to God our Savior, who daily bears our burdens"
—Psalm 68:19 (NIV).

One day before the blizzard of 2011 hit Oklahoma, I, along with the rest of the population, rushed to stock up on necessities. You would have thought it was the last minute Christmas rush to buy the perfect gift. In this case, it was comfort food for snowy weather.

Pushing my cart out the store's exit, I noticed that the area housing the shopping buggies was empty. I proceeded to the far end of the parking lot, what I call the back 40, and unloaded my groceries. As I was returning my cart to the corral, I noticed an older cowboy walking toward me. I informed him of the absence of buggies in the store and mentioned that he might want to take his own cart inside. Before he could answer, I noticed a pair of black rubber boots someone had left underneath a cart already pushed in place ahead of mine. About the time I said, "Someone forgot his boots," he rushed to reply, "Those are mine. I got about a mile up the road and realized I had forgotten them. I figured they'd already be gone."

Smiling, I helped him pull the carts apart so he could reach his forgotten merchandise. I said, "You'll probably need those if the weather gets as bad as they are predicting."

Agreeing, he said, "I just hope the snow doesn't get any higher than these boots are tall." Of course, I laughed and prayed that the weather forecasters were wrong this time. They weren't. Twenty inches of snow fell in this area with winds raging 20-25 miles per hour causing drifts to block the front doors to homes in the neighborhood. Weathermen proclaimed record snowfalls. I believe it and I bet the cowboy's rubber boots were shorter than the snow was deep.

It was day three before I ventured outside to shovel my driveway. Two hours later, I had it cleared but I couldn't go anywhere because the streets were still icy and snow packed. Very little traffic had moved through our neighborhood. Others experiencing cabin fever had escaped outdoors to sled, to clear their own driveways and to visit by shouting across the street. Some offered assistance, others advice.

When a neighbor proposed a trip to the store, I grabbed the chance to get out, restock shelves before the next storm hit and see for myself what the rest of the world looked like outside the confines of our world. Cars were in ditches; others slid along, barely missing another automobile or a stationary object. Good Samaritans stopped to help the stranded by pushing their vehicles out of the ditch.

A friend called later to ask for prayers for another Good Samaritan in her neighborhood. He had a heart attack while helping others clear their driveways. However, he didn't survive.

During trials, neighbors help neighbors and strangers offer assistance. No matter how tall our boots are the ones that God fills are the only size that can bear our burdens completely.

Have you sought His boots?

Jesus in Blue Jeans

"No one has ever seen God; but if we love one another, God lives in us and his love is made complete in us"—*1 John 4:12 (NIV).*

My back tires kept spinning. I tried putting my car in reverse and then drive, hoping to rock it out of the snowdrift I found myself stuck in during my escape attempt. Trying to get out of my neighborhood meant fleeing from the cabin fever I had caught while housebound. Instead, I had to depend on the kindness of four strangers who took pity on me, risking their own lives to help me get back on the road to safety. I never learned their names but I am grateful for their assistance.

Although the main roads were clear when I finally found freedom on the highway, my neighborhood streets were still hazardous. I should have stayed home. I didn't have an emergency. I had plenty of necessities at home. Like most, I had heeded the weather forecasters' advice and stocked up on everything.

Like others, I was also tired of being housebound. I had donned my snow boots, cleared my driveway, walked my dog through the drifts and visited with neighbors, offering assistance to those in need. I also thought I was competent enough to steer my vehicle on the winding roads that travel through my housing addition. Without the help of those Good Samaritans, I might have been stuck until the weather warmed up enough to melt the 20 inches of snow that shut down businesses, government and schools.

When circumstances force us to rely on others, maybe it is time to reflect on what it means to be like Jesus. News reports revealed stories of others who found themselves stranded, including five family members from out-of-state who had totaled their vehicle on the turnpike near our community. Passengers, including two adult women, and three small children, ranging in age from four months to two years, were caught in the storm on their way to Chicago, where the family was relocating to be near their mother. Local law enforcement assisted the family, bringing them back to the warmth of their headquarters before calling our pastor to request help.

Two church members left the comfort of their home to drive the group to a neighboring community to finish their trip by bus. However, the station had closed by that time. Jeff, and his wife Laurie, made sure the family was safely sheltered at a nearby motel before leaving. The stranded five were able to board the bus headed for Chicago the next day.

While I know of other good deeds during this record-breaking snowstorm, I also heard others complain that city and county crews were not doing enough. In our selfish human way, we forget that most are doing the best they can with what they have at their disposal.

When we remember Paul's words in Galatians 5:22-23, "But the fruit of the Spirit is love, joy, peace, forbearance, kindness, goodness, faithfulness, gentleness and self-control," we just might see Jesus in blue jeans.

What Good is Faith?

"The only thing that counts is faith expressing itself through love"
—*Galatians 5:6b (NIV)*.

What would you say if someone asked you, "What good is faith?" Would you relate your own experiences of faith in action? Maybe you would share your stories of answered prayers. Would you share with confident assurance the hope for what is going to happen in spite of the things we cannot yet see?

The following quote by minister and author, Pam Farrell, led me to research more about her and the meaning behind her words: "What good is a faith if you can't live it out?"

During my online search, I discovered more about Farrell and her husband, Bill, whose childhood backgrounds were anything but a fairy tale. Both of their family histories included alcoholism, anger issues and mental health problems. After meeting through a Campus Crusade for Christ event in college, the two eventually married and founded a relationship and marriage ministry.

The theme for the Farrell's ministry, flexibility and the priority of relationships was actually born out of a conversation Bill had with their oldest son. Bill says, "When Brock was three, he watched the Jesus video over and over. One day, he began to explain to me the process of beginning a personal relationship with Christ. I asked, 'Do you want to ask Christ to come into your life?'"

The three-year-old abruptly said, "No," then added, "As soon as Jesus gets out of the Bible, I will ask Him into my life." Making personal relationships real and practical has been the Farrell's driving force ever since.

The most pressing controversy in the early church was the relationship of new believers, particularly Gentiles, to the Jewish laws. In Galatians, the apostle Paul addressed this concern. He imparts God's guidelines to free believers from the burden of slavery so that each one might step into the truth. The apostle also tells the early Christians that freedom through Christ has freed us, not to do wrong, but to love and serve one another. As Christ's followers, Paul says that each one of us should carry another's burdens and be kind to each other.

How can we encourage others to make Jesus the Lord of their lives? How can we live out our faith? I like these suggestions by author Howard W. Hunter:

- Mend a quarrel.
- Seek out a forgotten friend.
- Dismiss suspicion and replace it with trust.
- Write a letter.
- Give a soft answer.
- Encourage youth.
- Manifest your loyalty in word and deed.
- Keep a promise.
- Forgo a grudge.
- Forgive an enemy.
- Apologize.
- Try to understand.
- Examine your demands on others.
- Think first of someone else.
- Be kind.
- Be gentle.
- Laugh a little more.
- Express your gratitude.
- Welcome a stranger.
- Gladden the heart of a child.
- Take pleasure in the beauty and wonder of the earth.
- Speak your love and then speak it again.

It is up to each of us to make Jesus come alive for others. After all, we are His hands and feet.

Are you living out your faith?

The Best How-to-Book Ever Written

"For I know the plans I have for you," declares the Lord, "plans to prosper you and not to harm you, plans to give you hope and a future. Then you will call on me and come and pray to me, and I will listen to you. You will seek me and find me when you seek me with all your heart"
— *Jeremiah 29:11-13 (NIV).*

How-to-books are great. However, if you're challenged by technical directions, as I am, it can be frustrating. Recently, after trading in my two-year-old cell phone for a newer model, I found myself stressing over the array of menu choices. This upgraded model has options I will never use but it was the least complicated in the store. The how-to-manual didn't help this technologically-challenged woman much, except to confuse her even more.

We live in a confusing, complicated world, moving at cyber-speed. Although technology has benefitted humanity in many ways, it has also led to what writer, Jon Gordon has observed as "a super-sized megadose of fear that pervades the hearts and minds of far too many people. This jumbo-sized fear can cause you to scurry in a million different directions or become paralyzed by it. In both cases, fear will lead you to take the negative road to failure."

Gordon asks his readers, "Do you know what fear and faith have in common?" His answer? "A future that hasn't happened yet."

When you examine the meaning of these two words, fear has negative implications and faith has positive associations. Which one would you choose? Since we cannot predict tomorrow, why worry about it? However, we can examine each situation and plan for the future, relying on God's guidance to help us make better decisions.

Now, if you haven't read the best how-to-book in the world, you are missing out on the answers for living your life in faith and hope instead of fear and despair. That book is the Bible and as Jeremiah 29:11 reveals, He does have a plan for each one of us, plans to prosper us and not harm us, but to give us hope and a future. However, if you read the two verses that follow this one, He also tells us to call on Him in prayer and He will listen. If we seek Him with all our heart, we will find Him.

Although I grew up in the church, I didn't seek Him with all my heart until I was in my late 40s. Driven by hopelessness of circumstances in my life, some of my own making and others not of my choosing, I prayed aloud for the first time, asking God for direction in my life. He answered my cries for help and for more than 10 years, I have been on a journey of hope, which began with His grace.

Continuing on His path, I turn each day to the best how-to-book ever written for guidance in one's daily life, a book with eternal consequences.

Have you read it? More importantly, have you studied it and asked God for guidance? The choice is yours.

Just Going Through the Motions

"Let us keep looking to Jesus. He is the author of faith. He also makes it perfect. He paid no attention to the shame of the cross. He suffered there because of the joy he was looking forward to. Then he sat down at the right hand of the throne of God"—*Hebrews 12:2 (NIRV).*

Have you ever felt you were just going through the motions of life? It's like putting your car on cruise control on a toll road. The scenery passes by, mile after mile, and by the time you arrive at your destination, you realize your eyes have never focused on anything worth remembering, especially if your route is a familiar one.

On a recent warm Saturday, I joined my sons and my grandchildren on a hike through a local nature preserve. Like me, they enjoy the outdoors, even when the trees are bare and the grass is brown. The spring shades of greens, yellows and other pastel colors had not yet made their debut but there was still plenty to experience and appreciate on a day made to be enjoyed.

Joy and delight are two words that come to mind when I watch my grandchildren get excited about God's creations. Each of the children was equipped with a cloth sack in which they had placed items like a notebook and pencil, snacks and bottles of water. My oldest granddaughter loves to draw so upon locating an animal track in the dried mud, she would squat down, pencil in hand and sketch the hoof or paw print left behind. After identifying the source of the track, she would then neatly print the animal species' name in bold letters.

Pine cones and acorns, not already claimed by squirrels, found their way into backpacks. Shiny rocks and fallen tree limbs became a source of play for young ones used to store-bought toys received on birthdays. Although I love nature, experiencing it through fresh eyes is a welcome respite from our complicated world.

Hiking through the woods that day, we could tell spring was near. Announcing its presence, a robin reminded us of the promise of new life to come and hope in the flowers that would soon spring forth from the dead winter earth.

In our lives, we can experience the same when we place our faith in the One who came to die for our sins. In most Christian traditions, Lent, the 40 days leading up to Easter, is observed. As Easter approaches each year, I find myself thinking about the death and resurrection of my Savior. He came with one purpose—to offer Himself as a sacrifice for the sins of humanity.

During Lent, I seek to spend more time with Jesus in the meadows of life and walk beside the peaceful streams with Him. I want my journey to be God-paced, full of simplicity but joy-filled as I tune out the monotony of a world gone crazy with commercialism and seek His presence.

If you're tired of going through the motions, seek the simplicity of a God-filled life.

Let's Get Real

"...if my people, who are called by my name, will humble themselves and pray and seek my face and turn from their wicked ways, then I will hear from heaven, and I will forgive their sin and will heal their land"
—*2 Chronicles 7:14 (NIV)*.

When I check out at a supermarket that offers me a choice of paper or plastic (bags), I don't hesitate before choosing paper. In the past, it would not have mattered but I get tired of seeing the landscape dotted with plastic bags that will take centuries to deteriorate. In the past, choosing paper meant a tree had been sacrificed. Now, paper recycling means less waste.

I know I could go one step further and use cloth bags; however, I don't really like remembering to bring them each time I go to the store. I do, however, recycle plastic bags and use them in my smaller trashcans at home. That soothes my conscience.

Did you know when we choose convenience over doing the "right" thing, it is hard to please God? We know what we should be doing. As Paul said in Romans 7:21-25, "I have discovered this principle of life—that when I want to do what is right, I inevitably do what is wrong. I love God's law with all my heart. But there is another power within me that is at war with my mind. This power makes me a slave to the sin that is still within me. Oh, what a miserable person I am! Who will free me from this life that is dominated by sin and death? Thank God! The answer is in Jesus Christ our Lord. So you see how it is: In my mind I really want to obey God's law, but because of my sinful nature I am a slave to sin."

While something we consider insignificant, like our choice of grocery bags, may not have eternal consequences, it is an example of the choices we must make each day. And choosing to follow God instead of our own sinful natures is one of the best decisions we can make.

For most of my adult life, I wasn't real because I wasn't perfectly honest with myself. I wasted too much of my time as a prisoner of "keeping up appearances." I was more concerned with what others thought of me than becoming the woman God created me to be. It took some life-changing experiences for me to seek His face.

Once we choose to follow our Savior, we no longer live in a plastic world created by man. Getting real with our Heavenly Father frees us to quit carrying around the anxieties of pretense, masking the person hiding behind it. He takes our sinfulness, our failures and our fears and places that load on the One who loves us and gave Himself for us. He makes all things new, including us.

Living in His reality is the answer to healing, not only in this world but also in the next. How real is God for you?

Soaking in God's Blessings

"I will make them and the places surrounding my hill a blessing. I will send down showers in season; there will be showers of blessing"
—Ezekiel 34:26 (NIV).

Although spring officially debuts with the vernal equinox in March, wildlife in my area was already preparing for this season when we celebrate new beginnings. Two days before the calendar and the weathermen announced the date, I removed a winter wreath from the storm door on the front of my house. I was puzzled at the change in its design until I realized that a bird had added her own décor with a nest. Since I was going to store the wreath in my garage, I removed her handiwork, but not without a tiny bit of guilt.

After tossing the nest in the trash, I replaced the wreath with one adorned in spring flowers. Several days later, a neighbor and his son were standing on my porch when I commented on the audacity of the bird that had homesteaded in my wreath. I glanced at my spring wreath and noticed a new nest. Before I could protest, the neighbor's son removed the nest and tossed it.

Two days later, I opened my front door to retrieve the morning newspaper. I was greeted by a fresh nest residing in my grapevine wreath. However, it wasn't empty. One tiny egg, about the size of the end of my thumb was nestled inside. I chuckled and made a promise to myself that I would not disturb nature again.

Since I had not seen the parents, I wasn't certain about the species of this tenacious bird, obviously in a hurry to get her nursery rebuilt. I called a friend who has worked on a nature preserve. After describing the egg and the nest, she determined that the squatters are house finches.

While I didn't invite them to share my house, I am enjoying the blessing of God's wonderful creation. My friend also shared more information about this bird species. She revealed that the mother would probably lay between four and five more eggs before she was finished. Further research about this species also revealed that the female constructs the nest—which explains the tenacious part.

The determination of this soon-to-be mother and the intricacy of the nest is a wonderful reminder of God's handiwork. I continued to watch as her family increased by four more tiny blue eggs. Relishing this glimpse of

God at work, it reminded me of many things in life that we take for granted or consider a nuisance.

Watching the preparations of the mother bird as she anticipated the birth of her young was a reminder to me to appreciate each day and what God has given us. I also occasionally remind my grown sons to cherish this time while their children are small because another birthday will pass and they, too, will leave home.

One day, Christians will leave this earthly home and join Jesus in our permanent home. In the meantime, I plan to soak in the sights and sounds of this home and the beauty of Gods' creation.

What about you?

Finding Lessons in Nature

"But ask the animals, and they will teach you, or the birds in the sky, and they will tell you; or speak to the earth, and it will teach you, or let the fish in the sea inform you. Which of all these does not know that the hand of the Lord has done this?"—*Job 12:7-9 (NIV)*.

Five small pale blue eggs filled the nest tucked inside the wreath on my front door. The mother, who constructed the nest three times, laid an egg daily. Previously, I mentioned this tenacious house finch who rebuilt her nest each time it was removed, the first time by me and the second time by a neighbor. However, the third time, as the saying goes, is a charm because she built her nest and laid an egg in the new abode before I discovered her plan. I didn't have the heart to remove it after I saw how determined she was to make my spring wreath her nesting place.

After I discovered the first egg, I cautiously approached her nursery each morning to check on developments. I tracked the mother's progress, after a friend suggested I document this unfolding saga with my camera. I became concerned because I had not caught her sitting on the nest; however, I knew she was tending the eggs because their positions in the nest changed each morning.

Even though I have always been fascinated with nature, I am amazed at the lesson I have learned from this tiny animal. She did not give up. Like our Creator, she is steadfast. She persisted and painstakingly reconstructed her nest for a third time. God never gives up on us either. No matter how many times we ignore the lesson He is trying to teach us, He is patient and persistent in His efforts.

I might not have given this mother bird's determination another thought until a friend reminded me that birds, using their beaks, pick up a twig, a blade of grass, small leaves or other debris, one at a time to create their masterpiece. "Try doing that with a pair of tweezers," my friend added, "or even better, put the tweezers in your mouth and try picking up one twig or blade of grass at a time."

After my friend's explanation, I began to appreciate even more the beauty of God's unique plans, including the tiniest of creatures we often take for granted. As I continued to wait for the five eggs to hatch, I began to ponder more lessons from our Heavenly Father.

While having lunch at a sidewalk café, I observed two birds fighting over a crust of bread. Their chatter reminded me of two selfish people, unwilling to share. However, the fight wasn't over as a third, then a fourth jumped into the fray. I smiled at their actions and I wondered, "Did they learn this greedy behavior from us?"

We can learn many lessons from the natural world if we take the time to notice. Are you open to what He is teaching you?

Are You Living in God's Fullness?

"I have come that they may have life, and have it to the full"
—John 10:10b (NIV).

Many of us, who love working in our yards and flowerbeds or walking in nature, feel closer to God when we take time to appreciate the beauty. I think it is because we feel His presence in each blooming flower, blade of green grass, the buzzing bees, the singing birds and even in the weeds that need pulling. I liken this love of nature to God's love for us. He created these things for us to enjoy, not to destroy. The weeds are a reminder to me that He wants to remove the bad stuff in our lives to make us more like Jesus.

Recently, while trimming my rose bushes, I noticed blood running down my forearms. I had on gardening gloves but could not bring myself to wear long sleeves. It was too warm. The thorns had ripped my flesh and as I watched the blood dripping from my arms, it was a reminder of Jesus' sacrifice for us.

His suffering is greater than anything I could ever imagine. The crown of thorns planted on His head caused more pain than what I felt from the barb of a rose bush. On a pilgrimage to Israel in 2010, I purchased an authentic Crown of Thorns, a vivid symbolic reminder of the suffering He endured for us.

Scripture tells us that the soldiers "platted a crown of thorns" or braided vines of thorns together to form a crown. According to my research, there are two types of thorn plants growing around the Holy Land. One is called the *Zizyphus Spina Christi* and the other *qundaul*. While both have long, flexible twigs that can be woven into crowns, the *qundaul* has the cruelest thorns of the two. The brutality of the soldiers has led most theologians to believe that the *qundaul* plant, with its spikes of 1 to 1 ½ inches long, was the one used for Jesus' crown of torture.

Can you imagine the pain and humiliation Jesus suffered at the hands of the soldiers? Why would their desire to mock Him lead to the weaving of a crown of thorns, a task that could have easily wounded their own bodies if they had been careless?

Careless is a word that applies to us if we are not aware of the thoughts, words and actions that can lead to our own destruction and others around us.

Our Savior hung painfully on a wooden cross with a crown of thorns pushed into His scalp. He endured it for me. He endured it for you. I believe it is no accident that spring and Easter coincide. Just as the flowers burst through the soil to reveal their beauty, our Savior rose from the dead three days after being killed in a manner most of us cannot comprehend. Friday was not the end. It was only the beginning. He came so that we may have life.

Are you living in God's fullness?

Where Would You Put It?

"God's blessing makes life rich; nothing we do can improve on God"
—Proverbs 10:22 (MSG).

"You can't have everything. Where would you put it?" This statement, by a well-known stand-up comic and actor, surprised me since his comedy is deadpan and surreal. However, I came across the quote at an inspirational Christian website that also publishes an uplifting magazine.

The comic's statement sparked a conversation with a friend. After going through a divorce and selling many family possessions, he realized life was much simpler without those trappings. My friend not only agreed we can't have everything, but he also said we don't need everything we want.

After selling a boat, a recreational vehicle, a large house with acreage and a barn, my friend explained that everything we possess can own us if we are not careful. I had never considered this aspect of ownership. He explained that when you own things, they require time and money to maintain. Even necessary possessions require maintenance, which takes time.

For seven years, I had an outdated computer repacked in its original box. I had moved three times since I purchased the equipment. It had been taking up space in my garage since I bought a new computer. I didn't like moving the dinosaur but I also wanted to erase the hard drive before I found someone who could use it. Eventually, I was able to get rid of it through a recycling program. Moving the computer each time I changed addresses cost me time, even though I was not maintaining it.

Maintaining a relationship with our Heavenly Father is a reminder that emptiness and dissatisfaction in life can't be cured with owning things. Each time I pack to move, I am amazed at how much I have accumulated. One of three things happens as I am packing. I give some of my treasured possessions away to friends or family, donate items to charity or have a garage sale. Most of the time, I do all three. Unless God decides to move me again, I am staying put.

Recently, I had both of my bathrooms repainted by a professional. As I removed the décor and necessities from each room to prepare for the painter, I scowled, realizing that once again, I had acquired more than I really needed. After the walls had dried, I made the decision to rid myself of unnecessary things.

As severe thunderstorms and tornadoes ripped through our state in mid-April, homes were destroyed, people were injured and lives were lost. Survivors were counting their blessings and not the loss of their possessions. Others were grateful for what they had left after the destruction.

Many people have been destroyed by their own greed. A recent article and photos in an area newspaper revealed a 12,000 square foot house to be auctioned off after the owner's desire to have it all led to his downfall.

When we learn that nothing we do can improve on God's blessings in our lives, then we become aware of how rich we really are.

Blessed are the Mothers

As Jesus was saying these things, a woman in the crowd called out, "Blessed is the mother who gave you birth and nursed you"
—Luke 11:27 (NIV).

All of us have at least one thing in common. We came into this world by way of a woman who gave birth to us. If we are blessed, our mother was there for us in times of trouble and joy. And, whether we wanted to learn them or not, she taught us many of life's lessons.

- My mother taught me foresight.
  "Make sure you wear clean underwear, in case you're in an accident."
- My mother taught me logic.
  "Because I said so, that's why."
- My mother taught me religion.
  "You'd better pray that will come out of the carpet."

I can recall my mother using some of these same tactics, which I also used on my own sons, along with many more. One lesson I taught was about the circle of life: "I brought you into this world and I can take you out." Raising sons was vastly different from raising two daughters, as my mother did.

However, can you imagine how Mary felt when she learned she was chosen to carry our Savior?

In his book, "Lost in Wonder, Love, and Praise," John Killinger says, "I believe in Jesus Christ, the Son of the living God, who was born of the promise to a virgin named Mary. I believe in the love Mary gave her Son, which caused her to follow Him in His ministry and stand by His cross when He died. I believe in the love of all mothers, and its importance in the lives of the children they bear. It is stronger than steel, softer than down, and more resilient than a green sapling on the hillside. It closes wounds, melts disappointments, and enables the weakest child to stand tall and straight in the fields of adversity. I believe that this love, even at its best, is only a shadow of the love of God, a dark reflection of all that we can expect of him, both in this life and the next. And I believe that one of the most beautiful sights in the world is a mother who lets this greater love flow through her to her child, blessing the world with the tenderness of her touch and the tears of her joy."

Mary didn't shed tears of joy at the crucifixion. She knew her Son's purpose. She had stored those things in her heart. She wept as she watched her Son die on the cross. However, even as Jesus was dying on the cross, He taught us a valuable lesson about mothers.

Henry Wadsworth Longfellow said it best, "Even He that died for us upon the cross, in the last hour, in the unutterable agony of death, was mindful of His mother, as if to teach us that this holy love should be our last worldly thought—the last point of earth from which the soul should take its flight for heaven."

Blessed are the mothers.

Can You Imagine the Possibilities?

*Jesus looked at them and said, "With man this is impossible,
but with God all things are possible"—Matthew 19:26 (NIV).*

For more than a decade, I had passed by a roadside business but had
never stopped to satisfy my curiosity. Some might not give the place a
second glance. If you are one of those who like the unusual and the
challenge of finding a treasure amidst junk, you might not have waited as
long as I did to stop and browse. Recently, two friends and I decided to
drive the 25 miles north of town to check out the interesting artifacts.

Driving through the gates of the business was like entering the past with a
touch of rust as well as the dented and tarnished. Organization was not
evident as there were piles here and piles there, which also describes my
desk when I am on deadline. Weeds and standing water vied for space with
relics from bygone eras. My friends and I tiptoed and stepped over the
remains of broken bicycles, rusty wheelbarrows and the skeletons of other
interesting, and sometimes, unidentifiable, fossils.

When an item captured my attention, I mentioned to my companions the
various ways to repurpose it. In most cases, with a little sanding or some
steel wool, some elbow grease and a can of spray paint, a treasure awaited
underneath the cast-off. While my friends marveled at my creative ideas,
neither was keen on the hard work it would take to restore them into an
objet d'art.

Did you know that Jesus is in the restoration business? He is in the
business of restoring us to completeness in our Heavenly Father. We all
have dents and dings from life's trials. Some of us have been abandoned by
those we trusted. Others, consumed with guilt, or the seeking of life's
pleasures, have turned away from God.

However, He never gives up on us. We're all under construction, a work-
in-progress. When we ask Jesus to take control of our lives, the process
begins. With grace as the transforming force, He gently removes the
tarnish and covers us with His unconditional love.

Isaiah 6:13 tells us, "He will give a crown of beauty for ashes, a joyous
blessing instead of mourning, festive praise instead of despair. In their
righteousness, they will be like great oaks that the Lord has planted for his

own glory." He will take the ashes of your life and turn them into something beautiful for His glory.

Imagine the possibilities of this transformation. His grace will direct your priorities to live for what matters. That transforming grace will help you to make wise decisions. In addition, His grace will allow you to experience real love, joy, peace, patience, kindness, goodness, faithfulness, gentleness and self-control.

However, you must make yourself available to be molded into the person He originally created you to be. His desire is to take us as we are and turn us into His masterpiece.

Sound impossible? Nothing is impossible with God.

Oh, what a Mess!

"Live clean, innocent lives as children of God, shining like bright lights in a world full of crooked and perverse people"—*Philippians 2:15b (NLT)*.

Although I enjoyed watching the tiny birds grow after hatching in the nest on my front door, I was equally glad when I could clean up the mess left behind. In mid-March, a finch built her nest in the wreath hanging on my storm door. Although she laid five eggs, only three hatched. Since the survivors grew to overflow the small nest, five would have really strained the seams of the carefully crafted abode.

As my three houseguests grew, so did the litter they made in my wreath and down the glass door front. I didn't want to disturb the siblings or their parents, so I had to bide my time until they learned to fly. For a recovering perfectionist and "clean-a-holic," it wasn't easy. Eight weeks, however, went by fast, as the bald-headed creations flourished into beautiful feathered creatures.

On the afternoon of the birds' departure, my grandchildren and I approached the front door to check on their progress. We were startled when all three flew from the nest. One after another, the finches zipped past our heads to freedom. My grandchildren were dismayed. And although I had become accustomed to peeking inside the nest each morning when I collected my morning newspaper, it was time for these wild birds to be free from the confines of the small world inside the silk flowers.

When I relayed the news of the birds' departure, and my eagerness to clean up the mess left behind, a neighbor cautioned me to leave the nest alone because she thought they would return. Her husband disagreed, believing that once they left their nesting place, they were gone for good.

Albeit longer and much more complicated, parenting is like that too. We give birth, we nurture our young, and then, hopefully, they mature, leave the nest and don't return. However, some of us are blessed to get a second chance at parenting when a grown child boomerangs back to the folds of a mother's apron. I am one of those mothers whose adult child returned home, not once but twice, until he found his wings. I know it was part of God's plan because both of us have grown during the process. I have jokingly told friends that I had cut the apron strings but my son kept tying them back together. However, I am joyful we had the opportunity to spend growing time together.

During the months my youngest son lived with me, I was able to model the message that God has created from the mess I had made of my life. At the same time, I have been pleased to see how my son is growing in Christ. Even though we, as parents, would like to keep our children from making mistakes, we have to let them experience the consequences of their choices.

Even if they make a mess of their lives, we must remember our Heavenly Father can also use it for His purposes.

Be with me, Lord, for Heaven's Sake

"The Lord has heard my cry for help;
the Lord will answer my prayer"—*Psalm 6:9 (NCV)*.

"Now I lay me down to sleep," according to my research, is a classic children's prayer from the 18th century. Although there are many versions, the following is an adaptation printed in "The New England Primer:" "Now I lay me down to sleep, I pray the Lord my soul to keep. If I die before I wake, I pray the Lord my soul to take."

As a child, I remember this version as the one painted on a small ceramic plaque that hung on my bedroom wall. The keepsake, passed on to my first grandchild, is more than 50 years old. While this prayer focuses on our nighttime prayers, the following one targets our mornings: "Now I wake me up to live; I'll give life all I have to give. If today I face a test, I'll cope and pray and do my best. With each breath and step I take, be with me, Lord, for heaven's sake."

While I start my morning with prayers, usually after preparing a mug of hot tea, I had never considered praying before I threw back the covers and climbed out of bed. My mornings are not as hectic as they once were. Since my children are grown and I am semi-retired, the early hours of the day are more peaceful. However, as the day progresses, life happens and stumbling blocks sometimes bring discouragement and frustration. When this happens, I recall this anonymous quote. "Lord, help me to remember that nothing is going to happen to me today that You and I cannot handle."

However, in the midst of trouble and pain, a simple one-word prayer is often the most heartfelt—Help! Does the brevity of a desperate plea bother God? I don't think so. He knows exactly what we need. Even if it is different from what we want, we must remember the outcome is in His hands. We may want immediate results while He is patiently teaching us a lesson.

I have seen prayers answered immediately and although God can still work miracles, usually His answer comes in more subtle ways. When I have faced trials, He has renewed my strength, given me an outpouring of hope or a peace that passes understanding. Those times have come in different ways, including the words of a friend, through reading scripture and prayer journaling, the kindness of a neighbor or even in the awesome beauty of nature. God's help varies but one thing that never changes is His faithfulness in answering our heartfelt prayers.

Our Heavenly Father is a great and present help in times of trouble. In the ever-changing circumstances of life, we can rest assured He is in control. Whether we are rising in the morning or going to sleep at night, we can count on His hearing our honest prayers.

With each breath and step we take, we know He is with us always.

How to Survive a Storm

"There will be a shelter to give shade from the heat by day,
and refuge and protection from the storm and the rain"
—*Isaiah 4:6 (NAS)*.

Massive tornadoes tore across our nation recently, pummeling communities, and leading to the loss of lives and property. The toll in deaths and damage will not end with the rebuilding of the areas affected by mass destruction. Changed forever by something completely out of their control, survivors will probably no longer take their lives for granted.

Storms, and not just those caused by the forces of nature, will happen. They are a fact of life. Disease, serious illnesses, accidents, divorce, death, unemployment, high gas prices and lost retirement savings are only a few of the things we have to weather in life.

Last month I planted three new trees in my yard. Because trees are vulnerable to nature's fury until their roots are established, I staked each one carefully. However, one of the trees is in an area of my yard that holds water when it rains heavily, leaving the ground spongy. After a recent powerful wind and rainstorm left this tree's roots exposed, I had to re-stake it with stronger posts. Hopefully, it will survive the stress.

Similarly, if our roots are not planted in Jesus, the storms of life will leave us wind-tossed and soaked in fear. In Matthew 8:23-27, we read of the disciples' fear when a severe storm arose at sea, covering the boat with large waves. Jesus was asleep. Think about that. Jesus was sleeping during a storm because He trusted His Father.

Matthew 25 says they woke Him by saying, "Lord! Save us! We are perishing!" Upon waking from His nap, He said to them, "Why are you afraid, O you of little faith?" Jesus then rebuked the winds and the sea, and it became calm. Of course, the men were astonished, saying, "What kind of a man is this One, that even the winds and the sea obey him?" Can you imagine the expressions on the 12 men's faces?

Although we can't see the people's faces, the audio portion captured by a convenience store's surveillance camera during the May 2011 Joplin tornado is haunting as 18 people huddled in a storage refrigerator during the twister's onslaught. Listening to the video, we can hear the powerful winds of the F5 tornado as it batters the store. Even above the deafening noise, however, you can hear a woman's voice crying out to Jesus to them. As far as I know, all who were crowded together in the small room survived the deadly storm.

We can survive the storms of life if our roots are planted firmly in His Word, for He is an ever-present help in times of trouble. In John 16:33, Jesus tells His disciples, "I have told you these things, so that in me you may have peace. In this world you will have trouble. But take heart! I have overcome the world."

With Jesus as our shelter, we can survive life's storms.

Just a Prayer Away

"God is our refuge and strength, an ever-present help in trouble"
—Psalm 46:1 (NIV).

With record heat for an Oklahoma June, flowers and gardens were already requiring more water. I dreaded getting my next water bill because I knew it would be higher than normal. With temperatures in the 90s and a relentless wind, vegetation, that had not had time to establish strong root systems, was suffering.

A phone call from a friend one morning reminded me that our lives are like the plant life that needs moisture to survive. My friend asked for prayer for a mutual acquaintance who is going through a difficult time in her life. Although this individual is a believer, she is overwhelmed by the hardships of a job loss, the loss of her home and the recent death of a friend. Without a church family to call her own, the burdens of her losses have left her without hope.

If I could bottle hope and give it to those who are without, it would come in the form of a meaningful and personal relationship with God. Through life's trials, I have learned that He is the only One who can give us the inner energy and strength to sustain us. If we want to tap into the special power that only He can provide, we have to engage in spiritual exercises, including prayer, Bible study and abiding in God's presence.

Even regular church attendance is not enough to nourish our roots. Some consider their Sunday morning ritual as a way to be spiritually fed or to socialize with like-minded individuals. However, living a life of hope requires work on our part. How can we feed our faith while waiting on Him? By believing and trusting the scriptures we read and about how our Heavenly Father works, our hope grows and we begin to understand the peace that passes all understanding.

Recently, I lost an expensive tree that I had been hesitant to purchase in the first place. After reading about its care, and making sure I selected a healthy one, I bought and planted the three-foot Japanese maple in my backyard. I have always admired their beautiful foliage but either the location or the soil in which it was planted did not agree with my small tree. Even though I thought I was fully prepared to care for this delicate maple, it did not survive.

The same is true in our lives. We need to be ready before trials come our way. Author Winnifred C. Jardine says, "Praying…is like sinking roots into the earth in search of water—living water. Sometimes the moisture

level is close to the surface and easy to reach, and prayers are quickly and obviously answered. Sweet relief! But oh, how often I have to push prayer roots down through hard layers of stubborn clay, deeper and deeper to find that nourishing water."

Our Lord is the living water. When we place our trust in Him, we learn that He is only a prayer away.

Are you seeking His living water?

Please Give Me a Drink

"If you knew the gift of God and who it is that asks you for a drink, you would have asked him and he would have given you living water"
—John 4:10 (NIV).

With temperatures in the triple digits, people, plants and pets were panting for life-giving water. On a hot, humid day, there's nothing better than a large glass of cold water, especially if you have been working, playing or exercising outdoors. The excess heat had already taken a toll on my annual flowers. With no rain in the forecast, their red, orange and yellow petals began to fade and wither.

While water covers 70.9 percent of the Earth's surface and is vital for all known forms of life, about 1.2 billion people live in areas where water is scarce. For those of us who can turn on a hydrant and cleanse our hands or stand in a shower to wash away the day's sweat and grime, water is a resource we take for granted. When we turn the handle, what do we expect? Without a second thought, we count on the flow of moisture from the tap.

When Jesus was returning to Galilee, He had to go through Samaria. Tired from His journey, He stopped at a well around noon to rest. However, He had nothing with which to draw water from the deep well. A Samaritan woman, who had come to draw water at a time when others were avoiding the midday heat, is startled when Jesus asks, "Will you give me a drink?"

Because Jews and Samaritans didn't associate at the time, the woman was curious to know why He would ask her for a drink. Jesus' reply was not what she expected. "If you knew the gift of God and who it is that asks you for a drink, you would have asked him and he would have given you living water."

Confused, the woman replied, "Sir, you have nothing to draw with and the well is deep. Where can you get this living water? Are you greater than our father Jacob, who gave us the well and drank from it himself, as did also his sons and his livestock?"

Imagine her puzzled look when Jesus answered, "Everyone who drinks this water will be thirsty again, but whoever drinks the water I give them will never thirst. Indeed, the water I give them will become in them a spring of water welling up to eternal life."

When the Samaritan woman requests the living water so she will never thirst again, Jesus reveals her past, acknowledging her five husbands and her current live-in. After this revelation, and further conversation, Jesus reveals His identity to the woman at the well.

We cannot survive very long without water. In hot conditions with no water, dehydration can set in within an hour. Plain and simple, humans need water to live. And, without the Living Water that Jesus offers, we merely exist.

Are you living or merely existing?

How Many Days Have You Lived?

"Teach us to number our days that we may gain a heart of wisdom"
—*Psalm 90:12 (NIV).*

Whether you are male or female, young or old, rich or poor, black, brown or white, we all have something in common. Our days are numbered. Even if we take good care of our bodies, eat healthy and exercise, and avoid those things detrimental to our health, we will all die someday. Sobering thought, isn't it?

None of us wants to dwell on when our last day will come because we really don't know. For those of us who have thought about it and long to be with our Savior, we still don't know when the last chapter will end.

Recently, I discovered a website about intentional living. The author offers a calculator at his site to determine how many days you have already lived and to forecast how many you have left based on a 70-year life span. Although the average lifespan for humans has continued to increase because of medical breakthroughs and other lifestyle improvements, only God knows the number of our days. Entering my birth date into the calculator, I discovered, as of this writing, that I have lived 21,050 days, nine hours and 19 minutes. However, as I continue writing, the hour and minutes will change. I am growing older as I write these words.

How many of us have said, "If I had only known then what I know now?" I certainly have. However, we cannot live with regret. Regret doesn't change the past but living intentionally can lead to a joy-filled life based on God's plan for us.

In Proverbs 2:1-6, King Solomon, the wisest man who ever lived said, "My son, if you accept my words and store up my commands within you, turning your ear to wisdom and applying your heart to understanding— indeed, if you call out for insight and cry aloud for understanding, and if you look for it as for silver and search for it as for hidden treasure, then you will understand the fear of the Lord and find the knowledge of God. For the Lord gives wisdom; from his mouth come knowledge and understanding."

When my sons were younger, I, like most parents, thought they were the smartest ones on the block. Now that I have grandchildren, I think they are even smarter. However, being smart and being wise are two different things. As a grandmother, I am wiser than when I raised my children. I have a multitude of experiences, both good and bad, on which to draw.

I have seen quotes to the contrary about wisdom and aging but King Solomon recognized his wisdom as a gift from God. In this sense, wisdom springs from a relationship with God. When we allow God access to our minds and our thoughts, living an intentional life means we are using each minute wisely. When we choose God's principles for life, we can say we have truly lived.

How will you live your days? Will it be in wisdom and joy?

Pointed in the Right Direction

"Point your kids in the right direction—when they're old they won't be lost"—Proverbs 22:6 (MSG).

On a mission trip to Costa Rica, our 30-person team included 10 children, ranging in age from nine to 18. All had accompanied their parents on the eight-day pilgrimage to assist with church construction and Vacation Bible School. From the youngest to the oldest, the youngsters were a blessing to the ones whom we had come to serve. However, as the week progressed, I realized how blessed our adult team members were by the presence of these younger missionaries.

Each young person connected with the Hispanic children who attended our daily VBS. Language was not a barrier. Whether toddler or teen, all were united through song, stories, scripture, crafts, games and snacks. Smiles and laughter erupted throughout the two-hour sessions as they shared a common bond—a love for our Lord.

Just as the Costa Rican children were encouraged by their parents or other adults to attend church and participate in VBS, our young people have learned about the love of God. However, they have also learned how to translate that love into action. By accompanying their children on a journey of more than 2,000 miles to serve others in a different country, these parents are pointing their children in the right direction.

Encouraged by the path I see my grandchildren following, I love sharing how God is working in their young lives. Recently, my two oldest grandchildren were playing dress-up at my house. When they grew quiet, I discovered them in my guest bedroom. Brennan, who is six, was sitting in a small wooden chair while his eight-year-old sister, Cheyenne, was perched on the edge of the bed. When I inquired about their play, Cheyenne replied, "We're playing church. Brennan is the preacher."

Amused, I asked my grandson about the topic of his sermon. His reply? "God is my hero." This grandmother's heart danced with hope and delight at the scene before her, as well as the words my grandson spoke. However, the moment wasn't over. Cheyenne said, "Nana, we were getting ready to sing some songs but we're not sure which one."

I suggested, "Jesus Loves Me," and "If You're Happy and You Know it." I joined in as they enthusiastically clapped, stomped and shouted, "Amen." I know my grandchildren are headed in the right direction.

A recent sermon by a well-know television pastor focused on the power of praying mothers and grandmothers. Money cannot buy the best gift we can give our children and grandchildren, which is to know the love of Jesus Christ.

Andrew Murray said, "God gave us the greatest proof of love that the world has ever seen." Murray, who died in 1917, was a South African writer, teacher, and Christian pastor. Murray considered missions to be "the chief end of the church."

While it is wonderful to go on mission trips overseas, our first mission in life is to teach our children the way they should go…"when he is old, he will not turn away from it."

Are you pointing your children in the right direction?

Don't Close Your Eyes

"So do not fear, for I am with you; do not be dismayed, for I am your God. I will strengthen you and help you; I will uphold you with my righteous right hand"—*Isaiah 41:10(NIV).*

Have you ever closed your eyes when you were afraid? Did it help? Did it make the fear disappear? Depending on your fear, closing your eyes may not be an option.

Closing my eyes was not an option when I decided to work on overcoming my acrophobia. If you have a fear of being at a great height, then you also suffer from the same malady. I don't know when or why I started dreading heights. Someone recently told me that it is not a fear of heights but a fear of falling, which makes more sense.

What doesn't make sense to me was the feeling that overcame me when I interviewed an 80-year-old woman who parachuted from an airplane to celebrate her birthday. I was present when she did a tandem jump in 2001. After she reached the ground safely, I asked her how it felt. Her description of the experience left me, a woman afraid of heights, with a desire to do the same thing.

Since then, I have worked gradually to overcome my acrophobia. My first step was to get over my fear of climbing the ladder into my attic. Two years later, I rode in a bucket truck to shoot a photo of 400 teenagers on a football field. I never asked how high, I just trusted God that I wouldn't fall.

On a mission trip to Costa Rica several years ago, I took another leap of faith when our team members took a day off from construction to see the sights and enjoy a zip line through the rain forest. If you are not familiar with a zip line, it requires being physically attached to a cable by wearing a harness, which attaches to a removable trolley. A helmet and thick leather gloves are also required.

As I climbed the steps to begin the course, I was excited. I thought, "I can do this." Of course, the first line was not that high. Each line, however, became progressively higher as we zipped through the forest. At one point, we were approximately 300 feet in the air. Although I knew I was attached to the overhead line, zipping over the treetops at a high rate of speed was somewhat out of my comfort zone, especially when I overcorrected on one line and had to pull myself about seven feet to reach the platform.

However, I never closed my eyes. I kept my eye on the goal, which was the next platform because I was afraid my fear of heights would lead me to panic. I could see the scene below me only through my peripheral vision.

How often do we take our eyes off God, allowing fear to take us places we never intended to go? Fear can paralyze us but God's strength will uphold us.

Don't close your eyes. You'll miss the journey.

Why You Need to Share Your Story

"Let the redeemed of the Lord tell their story— those he redeemed from the hand of the foe, those he gathered from the lands, from east and west, from north and south"—Psalm 107:2-3 (NIV).

Do you know the greatest love story ever told? You might begin your list with those from literature, movies and even historical figures, like Cleopatra and Mark Antony, Lancelot and Guinevere, Scarlet O'Hara and Rhett Butler or maybe Romeo and Juliet. However, the greatest love story involves you.

It is the story of your Savior, who sacrificed His life for you. Is there any greater love than that? He loved us to death. Could you do that? Would you be willing to give up your life for another?

Scripture tells us that in this life we will have many troubles. In John 16:33, Jesus says, "In this world you will have trouble. But take heart! I have overcome the world."

Many times, we try to climb those mountains of trouble alone. We forget that we have someone who has already conquered our obstacles. If the mountain were smooth, you couldn't climb its slippery slope. It's while we are still in the valley, trying to climb up that mountain of hope, that we really grow in our faith.

Part of spiritual growth includes sharing our stories with others. Our stories of overcoming hardships and choosing the right path can encourage others as they struggle with their own journey. It is in the sharing of our story that we are also strengthened for the next leg of our own travels through life. Along the way, our sharing brings hope to others. When we hear another's story, it, along with its message, becomes a part of who we are. Somewhere as we traverse the crooked roads of life, we may find their story's value in the significance it brings to ours. It is about sharing in each other's humanity.

Recently, I went with a friend to see the movie, "The Help." Set in 1960s Mississippi, the movie is the story of a southern society girl who returns from college resolved to be a writer. After landing a job as a columnist for the local newspaper, she decides to write a book based on interviews with black women who have spent their lives taking care of prominent southern families. After much persuasion, the black women agree to share their stories of discrimination and hardship with Eugenia "Skeeter" Phelan. The women, however, realize that their names must be changed in the story for their own protection. Skeeter must also write under the guise of "anonymous." The sharing of their stories does two things. It brings hope to the black community and gives Skeeter the courage to pursue her dreams.

Author Melody Beattie once said, "Live your life from your heart. Share from your heart. And your story will touch and heal people's souls." Everyone has a story to tell. Although we may have arrived at our current destination by a different route, a common thread runs through each one.

Have you shared your story?

Are You Living an Intentional Life?

"The purposes of a person's heart are deep waters, but one who has insight draws them out"—*Proverbs 20:5 (NIV).*

Have you ever been required to complete an inventory? Maybe it was on the job and you had to compile a listing of merchandise or stock on hand, including a detailed, descriptive list of articles giving the code number, quantity and value of each. Maybe it wasn't quite that specific but you were accountable for the final results.

When I was a high school librarian, one of my duties was to help complete an end-of-the-school year inventory of all the library's holdings. Thank goodness, we eventually purchased a hand-held scanner to read each bar code as we moved around the large room of approximately 12,000 books. Previous years required a more intensive process to complete the task. With the new technology, the inventory was completed in less than 10 days.

As a public school teacher for 30 years, I also encouraged students to set goals for their lives, starting with what they hoped to accomplish that school year. They were asked to break them down into bite-size pieces. However, my ultimate goal was to help them see that what they put into their studies would affect them the rest of their lives. If they chose to not complete assignments, study for tests or attend classes regularly, they would not be successful. It was an individual choice to pass or fail.

In his book, "The YOGOWYPI Factor: You Only Get Out What You Put In," author Bill Cordes discusses the wisdom of our mission, which allows us to define our purpose and mission. He gives a four-step process of the wisdom of mission. He says, "Wisdom of mission defines what happens to us, both internally and externally, when we have a dream of pursuing something bigger than ourselves."

Pursuing something bigger than ourselves means making conscious choices that bring joy to our hearts as well as to the hearts of others. Called intentional living, it means to do things with intention and on purpose. Sometimes that requires an inventory of where we are and where we want to be in life, instead of letting the wind blow us whichever way it chooses.

Making choices like Harry and Agnes of Snohomish, Washington, who, when they got married, intentionally decided to have a strong family life. After having children, the couple built a summer cabin on a small island where they played games and spent time together. They also demonstrated an intentional life by praying and showing Christian love to others. Moreover, when the couple died, the family didn't stop gathering.

Before she died, Agnes said, "I've done everything I wanted to do. I have no regrets." At her funeral, the pastor said, "Our time on earth is limited, and God calls us to be good stewards by living intentionally. That means using everything we have … in ways that would delight God so, at the end of our lives, we might have no regrets."

Are you living an intentional life? *Don't forget the YOGOWYPI Factor.*

Lessons from a Lawnmower

"However, you were taught to have a new attitude. You were also taught to become a new person created to be like God, truly righteous and holy"—Ephesians 4:23-24 (GWT).

I pulled the starter but nothing happened. I had filled it with gas and checked the oil. I tried repeatedly; still nothing happened except for a small sputter. My lawnmower had only been used two summers. My previous push mower, of the same brand, had lasted seven summers. I was frustrated. I needed to mow my lawn before I had to hire someone to bale it. Recent rains had left my Bermuda grass luscious enough for cows to make a meal of it. That thought crossed my mind but I didn't want to clean the mess they would leave behind.

I pushed the contrary machine back into the shed until a mechanically-inclined neighbor could solve the problem. I then borrowed another neighbor's mower, only this one does not require gas or oil. It doesn't have a starter either. It requires old-fashioned muscle power. My maternal grandmother had one and, as a child, I loved to mow her lawn when I visited. Now, I was transported into the past while pushing my neighbor's newer version through the grass.

As I mowed, I recalled my earlier frustration with my dead mower. I decided not to worry about it, nor dwell on the fact that mowing would take longer to finish. My power mower was not self-propelled but it was easier to push than the reel mower requiring frequent stops to dislodge a clump of thick grass or a stick caught in the blades. Instead, I began to count my blessings.

I had neighbors whom I could count on to help me out. One loaned me her mower and I knew the other one would be able to diagnose and fix mine at no charge. I also realized the benefits of free exercise. I didn't have to go to the gym to work out that day. I could feel the calories dripping off me, along with the perspiration that rolled down my face and back. I also knew I was blessed to have a lawn to mow, even if it was tall enough to hide ostrich eggs.

Pushing the reel mower also made me appreciate individuals, like my grandmother, who didn't have a choice. She not only mowed with one of these motorless machines, she grew a huge garden each year and canned the produce.

My thoughts also wandered to a man at our church who had passed away at age 94. Matthew never complained but always had a smile on his face. Even though he couldn't do the things he had been able to do in the past, he was an inspiration to all who met him, including me. Reading his obituary, I learned that although retired, he had continued to help others do electrical work into his early 80s.

If you think you're too old to learn a new lesson, consider the simple lawnmower. I've discovered it's all about attitude and perspective.

Three Secrets to Managing Life

"Preach the word; be prepared in season and out of season; correct, rebuke and encourage—with great patience and careful instruction"
—*2 Timothy 4:2 (NIV).*

When I came across the following quote: "There are three secrets to managing. The first secret is having patience. The second is being patient. And the third most important secret is patience," I wanted to know more about the person behind this statement, Chuck Tanner.

Tanner, who passed away this past February at age 82, was the popular manager of the Pittsburgh Pirates. He died just days before his team was set to open spring training. While I don't claim to be a baseball expert, I was intrigued by the on-line information that painted the picture of a man who was greatly admired by his players, friends and fans.

In a 2002 interview, knuckleballer Wilbur Wood, who played for Tanner when he managed the White Sox in the 70s, briefly described what it was like to play for Tanner: "Chuck was the most positive guy I've ever been around. No matter how bad things were going, Chuck would always find something to be positive about, something to try to keep you going. In fact, Chuck spent more time with guys who were having trouble or in a slump than with guys who were doing well. I thought that was really smart. Remember, in baseball you only have 25 guys; if two or three guys are down or having a hard time suddenly your roster is really short. Chuck tried to keep everybody ready to play because that gave us a better chance of winning."

For Chuck Tanner, managing a baseball team wasn't just about winning. Among his many memorable quotes about the profession is this: "I don't think a manager should be judged by whether he wins the pennant, but by whether he gets the most out of the twenty-five men he's been given."

In Paul's letters to Timothy, he encourages the young disciple to fight the good fight. His goal was to get the most out of this young man who had chosen to follow Jesus. Timothy, who is shy and unassertive, has become discouraged because of the false teachers who have infiltrated the church. However, Paul understands the importance of training Timothy, who will one day take his place as a church leader. Paul's guidance, just like that of Chuck Tanner, requires patience.

Tanner said, "I communicated individually and collectively, and I was the boss. I treated everybody the same. Every day was a new day. No matter what transpired that day, if I hollered at you, no matter what happened, the slate is clean the next day. We're all starting new. That's the perspective I kept, and that's the way I treated everybody."

God is like that, too. He is patient with us. Each day, He gives us the opportunity to start over. His mercies are new each morning.

The secret to managing life is about doing life God's way, with patience, perseverance and prayer.

Let God Have Your Mess

"Praise be to the God and Father of our Lord Jesus Christ, the Father of compassion and the God of all comfort, who comforts us in all our troubles, so that we can comfort those in any trouble with the comfort we ourselves receive from God"—*2 Corinthians 1:3-4 (NIV).*

If you've ever spilled something sticky on the floor, you know how difficult it can be to eliminate all traces of the mess. You can sop it with a paper towel, scrub it out of the cracks, hand wash it with a cleaner, mop it with even more cleansers and still find your feet sticking to the floor when you walk across it barefooted.

In a hurry to leave for a trip, I wanted to make sure my hummingbirds had enough to eat. I filled two feeders. Headed to the door with the second one, I felt it slipping from my grasp. In spite of my juggling efforts, the glass feeder fell, shattering on the floor. In my dash to get everything done, I had made a mess, a very sticky one, and one I had to clean up before I left.

Our lives can be just like that bird feeder, destroyed by carelessness. While we make mistakes and accidents happen, there are times we make wrong choices leading to messes we can't clean up. We can't grab a towel, a broom or a mop to swipe, sweep or sponge away the dirt. No amount of scrubbing can make the pain and destruction disappear. We might try to sweep it under the rug but it will always reappear like dust bunnies hiding beneath the bed.

In our messiness, we sometimes forget there is someone who is bigger than our messes. In the middle of that mess, we might feel unwanted, unloved and unworthy. However, it doesn't matter how big the mess, God still wants you. The Bible is full of stories about adulterers, cowards, murderers, prostitutes and thieves. God changed them. He used them for His glory. King David, who broke most of the Ten Commandments, was called a man after God's own heart.

What about Moses, who was shy and a murderer? Then there was Noah, who was a drunkard. Abraham was a liar. Jacob was a cheater. What about Paul, a former religious terrorist whom God used for His purposes? When Jesus picked his 12 disciples, did he say, "Clean up your lives and then find me?" No, he simply said, "Come follow me."

When the prodigal son returned home, did his father turn him away? I'm sure his mess was evident from the pig stench. Instead of telling him to clean up first, his father welcomed him home with open arms.

Titus 3:5 says, "He saved us, not because of righteous things we had done, but because of his mercy. He saved us through the washing of rebirth and renewal by the Holy Spirit…"

When we let God have our mess, He cleans it up from the inside out. His plans are for good and not for disaster. He wants to give us hope and a future.

Have you given Him your mess?

What's Stuck in Your Head?

"Is anyone among you in trouble? Let them pray. Is anyone happy?
Let them sing songs of praise"—*James 5:13 (NIV)*.

Have you ever had a song stuck in your head? The refrain goes through your mind over and over until it drives you crazy. Maybe it's the jingle on a television commercial or a popular song with a catchy tune. Can you remember the Oscar Mayer jingle or the "Gimme a break," Kit Kat commercial? Maybe it's the "The Lion Sleeps Tonight" from the movie "The Lion King" that has wormed its way into your brain? "In the jungle, the quiet jungle, the lion sleeps tonight. A-wimoweh, a-wimoweh, A-wimoweh, a-wimoweh."

Did you know the English language even has a term for this phenomenon? It's called an "earworm." According to the dictionary, an earworm is a song or tune that gets stuck in one's mind and repeats as if on a tape. Other terms include cognitive itch **or** sticky tune. I wonder how you can scratch an itch in your brain.

I had never heard of the term "earworm," until I came across it when another writer used the word in a devotional. I wanted to learn more so I "googled" the term. Nearly 98 percent of people have had songs stuck in their head, according to the Society for Consumer Psychology. Research of a sample population revealed, on average, the episodes last over a few hours, with women being significantly more annoyed than men with the stuck song syndrome.

Although researchers say there is no cure, many people battle the "itch" by using another tune to force out the irritating worm. Others try to finish the song in their heads to end the cycle. Participants in a well-documented survey reported using all sorts of techniques for trying to get rid of earworms but generally fighting the earworm just made it stronger. Psychologists have discovered that thought suppression can be counter-productive. The harder you try to suppress the worm, the stronger it can become.

Worrying is much like that earworm and it can suck the life out of you. We worry about so many things that never happen. According to a "Scientific American" article, "Why We Worry," our chronic tendency to worry originates from a craving for control. We want complete control of everything that happens or might happen in our lives. Constantly focusing on our worries makes it worse, just like that earworm that won't give up until we acknowledge it. If we allow fear to dominate our lives, it can become chronic and debilitating.

So, what's the answer? According to Philippians 4:6-7, "Do not be anxious about anything, but in every situation, by prayer and petition, with thanksgiving, present your requests to God. And the peace of God, which transcends all understanding, will guard your hearts and your minds in Christ Jesus."

As James tells us in chapter five, if we're in trouble, pray. If we're happy, sing songs of praise.

Don't let worries worm their way into your head.

What's Your WOW Factor?

"For ever since the world was created, people have seen the earth and sky. Through everything God made, they can clearly see his invisible qualities—his eternal power and divine nature. So they have no excuse for not knowing God"—*Romans 1:20 (NLT).*

Retrieving the morning newspaper, just as dawn is breaking on the horizon, is a wonderful reminder of God's love for me. Recently, the red, orange and purple sunrise was so spectacular, I couldn't help but say, "Wow!" My next words were, "Thank you, God."

The word, "wow," has its roots as a Scottish interjection from 1513, and means "a natural expression of amazement." What could be more natural or amazing than seeing God's creation at its best? I've always loved the outdoors and have been fascinated with nature since I could walk. As a child growing up in Louisiana, I recall spending hours searching for frogs, playing with roly-poly bugs, capturing fireflies in a jar, making chains from clover flowers, picking blackberries on the 60 acres my daddy leased or just lying on my back in the grass, trying to discover shapes in the clouds.

Even though it has been about three years, I can still recall the thrill of discovering a tiny purple flower pushing its head through the dead earth of late March. Nothing else was blooming. No green grass announced the upcoming onslaught of spring rains. Why does that small colorful vegetation still impress itself in my memory? It was an Easter afternoon when I was hiking through the woods with my family and a small reminder of His love.

As I was out walking my dog this morning, the wind rustled the grass in a nearby field. I stopped, closed my eyes, and imagined God's whisper of love in the gentle breeze. I recalled another time when I felt the powerful presence of the Lord. During a pilgrimage to Israel two years ago, our group traveled by boat across the Sea of Galilee. After the engines were shut off, we closed our eyes as a breath of fresh air rocked the wooden boat. The only word that came to mind was "wow," as tears spilled down my cheeks. I could imagine Jesus walking across the water toward our vessel.

Many companies and advertising firms use the phrase "The WOW Factor." I "googled" the words and discovered 29,500,000 results for that term.

Many companies and advertising firms use the phrase "The WOW Factor." I "googled" the words and discovered 29,500,000 results for that term.

However, their idea of "wow" and God's are vastly difference. While businesses want to separate consumers from their hard-earned dollars, God wants to impress upon us how powerful He is. He is a God who created the entire universe, from the largest creature to the most miniscule of life.

"Wow" is not about the latest technological gadgets, although they do have their place, but about what our Heavenly Father has done for each of us. He not only created the heavens and the earth and everything upon it, He also sacrificed His only Son for our sins. I cannot wrap my mind around a God who would do that for me.

Can you?

His Word Endures Forever

"All people are like grass, and all their glory is like the flowers of the field; the grass withers and the flowers fall, but the word of the Lord endures forever"–1 Peter 1:24-25 *(NIV)*.

Working in my flowerbeds brings me pleasure. Not only do I like getting my hands dirty in the soil, I like the reward that comes from my effort. When bushes grow, seeds sprout and flowers bloom, I see the results of my hard work. The benefits of their beauty are a bonus.

Last spring, I purchased a packet of Morning Glory seeds at a local dollar store. I had never had any luck growing this very fast-growing annual vine known for its trumpet-shaped flowers, which come in blue, pink, purple, scarlet, white and multicolored blooms, attracting hummingbirds, bees, ladybugs and butterflies.

Blooms open in the cool of the morning, hence, the name Morning Glory. During the fall, flowers open all day. They usually bloom from summer until fall frost. My Morning Glory plant grew fast, covering my brick mailbox with its profuse vine. However, I was disappointed when it didn't bloom in the summer. I had watered it, fertilized it and waited for the flowers to appear. Several neighbors had also planted seeds next to their mailboxes. While out walking my dog each day, I enjoyed the flowers growing abundantly on their vines.

According to the information I had read about this flower, the vines die with a winter frost but will reseed themselves each year. However, my vine had not produced any flowers. Although I had only spent a buck plus tax for the packet of seeds, I had looked forward to seeing its blooms. The morning after our first heavy frost in mid-October, I went out to retrieve my mail. I was amazed when I noticed several buds on the vines not destroyed by the frost.

Excited about my discovery, I immediately called a neighbor with whom I had lamented about my bloomless vine. Like me, she couldn't believe the vine had bloomed after a frost. In this instance, seeing is believing.

Each morning, I admire the flowers that now open daily to greet the sun as well as me when I visit my mailbox. Viewing their purple flowers is a reminder to me that God never gives up on us, even if we turn away from Him.

Revisit the Bible stories to see how many times God was disappointed by humanity's behavior. Men and women turned away from Him repeatedly and continued to sin. When God chose Noah to build the ark, then flooded the earth, destroying the rest of the world's inhabitants, He also made a promise in the form of a rainbow as a reminder that He would never do it again.

When Abraham and Sarah grew impatient after God promised them a son, they took things into their own hands. Abraham had a son by his wife's servant. God could have changed His mind after this disobedience. However, He didn't.

Just as my late-blooming flowers bring hope, so does God's Word. It endures forever.

Let's Fight 'Christmas Creep'

"Do not store up for yourselves treasures on earth, where moths and vermin destroy, and where thieves break in and steal. But store up for yourselves treasures in heaven, where moths and vermin do not destroy, and where thieves do not break in and steal. For where your treasure is, there your heart will be also"–*Matthew 6:19-21 (NIV).*

Have you ever heard the expression "values are caught, not taught?" I had never heard this phrase before. After coming across those words in one of my devotional readings, I began to think about it and I asked myself, "What are we teaching the next generation?"

As a child growing up in the 50s and 60s, I recall three separate holidays between October 31 and December 25. I can recall trick-or-treating for UNICEF, a global humanitarian relief organization providing children with health care and immunizations, clean water, nutrition and food security, education and emergency relief in over 150 countries. I can remember taking the box provided by the organization and collecting coins along with Halloween candy. We returned the money in the small cardboard box to our church, which sponsored the drive.

Then, there was Thanksgiving with the turkey and all its trimmings. It was a time to be thankful for all we had and to help those who had less. Our church youth group, as well as the Camp Fire girls, collected canned goods for those in need.

We didn't begin thinking about Christmas shopping or decorating until at least a week after Thanksgiving. Now, pumpkins and Christmas trees fight for shelf space at the same time, all in late September. You have to really search for anything resembling Thanksgiving décor because it gets lost between the ghosts and goblins and Santa Claus. What happened to Thanksgiving? Now, early birds dream of Black Friday instead of a white Christmas.

I heard another new term recently, this time on a radio station. It's called "Christmas creep." When I "googled" the expression, I came across a recent article titled "Shoppers urged to fight 'Christmas creep,'" written by a "South Florida Business Journal" reporter. She said, "For some, it's a way to get into the holiday spirit. But, for many, it's simply too early – and even distasteful." I have to agree.

The reporter also cited instances of some retailers beginning their Christmas season promotions as early as July. In November 2005, when I wrote my first column, titled "Too Many Presents under the Tree," businesses were putting out Christmas décor, earlier and earlier. At the time, I recall the words of a sales associate at a local store who predicted this trend. After my comment to her about the early arrival of the Christmas season in October, she replied, "Next thing you know, we'll be putting stuff out in July."

Our culture, if we allow it, can teach us the wrong values. However, if we model Jesus' words in Matthew 6:19-21, we realize that material things have no real value.

Family, friends, good health, and enough to meet our needs is what life is really all about.

Not My Job...or is It?

"I desire to do your will, my God; your law is within my heart"
–Psalm 40:8 (NIV).

Have you ever asked someone, maybe a colleague at work, to help with a project, only to hear, "That's not my job" or something similar? Have you ever answered with that same reply when someone has asked you for help?

I have never, at least not that I can recall, used that excuse for not helping someone. On second thought, I believe I have. However, that was BC or before Christ in my life. When He takes up residence in your heart, you see people and situations in a different way. It doesn't happen overnight. It happens when you listen to that still, small voice directing you to do the right thing.

With the holiday season upon us once again, it is time to re-examine what really matters and it's not about you or me, for that matter. Whether you're a shop-till-you drop gift buyer or one who gets in and out of a store faster than gas prices going up during the holidays, I think we need to be reminded of some common courtesies that actually have their basis in the Word.

Have you ever been shopping, whether during the holidays or not, and realized before you reached the checkout there was an item you didn't need or want? Or maybe, your wants were bigger than your pocketbook and instead of walking across the store to return the item to its proper spot on the shelf, you deposit it in an unlikely place. I've found perishable food stashed in electronics. I guess someone decided a new television was more important than eating.

Let's examine this further. If we have a tendency to gain weight during the holidays, wouldn't it be wiser, as well as more polite, to push your cart across the store to place the unwanted item back in its proper department? You'll be burning calories and saving time for a harried store employee. Remember Luke 6:31? "Do to others as you would have them do to you."

The Golden Rule also applies to the return of shopping carts after we have unloaded purchases into our automobile. Yes, the store employs people who gather the empty buggies and wheel them back inside for other shoppers. However, let's make it our duty to push our empty cart into the nearest corral where the employee can round them up for an easier trip back to the store. Those carts don't roll themselves back inside without help.

I've heard shoppers say, "That's what they pay these people to do." Why do the stores have the cart corrals in the first place? The main reason is to keep the four-wheeled metal baskets from escaping and rolling across the parking lot where they can damage someone's vehicle—and it just might be yours someday. So, set an example. Read 1 Corinthians 11:1. "Follow my example, as I follow the example of Christ."

Wouldn't the world be a better place if we all practiced the Word?

Seeking His Presence this Holiday Season

"You make known to me the path of life; you will fill me with joy in your presence, with eternal pleasures at your right hand"–*Psalm 16:11 (NIV)*.

"Dashing through the aisles, steppin' on people's toes, oh' what fun it is to fight the Christmas rush."

Okay, I am neither a singer nor a songwriter but I wanted you to feel the urgency that many of us feel at this time of year. While the commercial blitz started weeks before Thanksgiving, advertisements are urging us to spend, spend, spend with promises of promotions that won't last any longer than the new toy your child finds under the tree on Christmas morning.

I may sound cynical and some of you might say I'm a scrooge. I'm not. I love this time of year but I've never found it exciting to fight crowds just to save money on a gift. I also am dismayed when I hear of shoppers' rudeness and lack of consideration for a fellow human being. In the past, I let the expectations of others dictate my actions during the holidays until the real reason for Christmas settled in my spirit.

I love finding the right present that will bring a smile to a loved one's face. After all, didn't our Heavenly Father give us the best gift of all? Who is this man called Jesus? Why did He choose to spend time on earth for 33 years before He made the greatest sacrifice of all? Why is it important for me, and for you, to know Him and not just know "of Him?"

The answer is in God's Holy Word. In the Contemporary English Version, John 3:16 says, "God loved the people of this world so much that he gave his only Son, so that everyone who has faith in him will have eternal life and never really die."

We can get so busy during this time of year with Christmas parties and baking, shopping for the right gifts and trying to be everything to everyone that we forget the One who made this all possible. God created us. Not only that, He loves us so much that He wants us to know Him now so we can spend eternity with Him. Jesus came so that each of us could know and understand our Heavenly Father in a personal way. Jesus alone is the One who can bring meaning and purpose to life.

Even during the busiest moments of our Christmas preparations, God wants to come to us in the midst of everyday life. May I suggest slowing down and inhaling His goodness during your shopping? Stop. Become aware of your actions and thoughts. Ask Him to be in the moment with you.

Our calling, as believers, is to be radically different, especially at Christmas with which our culture is obsessed. By stopping, listening and realizing that acquisitions can be a distraction from life, we can come before our Heavenly Father filled with joy.

Are you seeking His presence during this season?

Let There Be Peace on Earth

"Glory to God in the highest, and on earth peace among those with whom he is pleased"– *Luke 2:14(ESV).*

Although I am not a history buff, I love stories that speak to the heart. Memorizing dates or studying the intricacies of war doesn't appeal to me. However, the personal stories of the people attached to history do intrigue me. Recently, I came across a story that took place in the midst of the fiercest fighting of World War I.

The story, recalled by those who were there, occurred around Christmas time when a German soldier began singing "Stille Nacht." His solo erupted into a chorus as he was joined by English voices singing "Silent Night." Following this carol, a British regiment serenaded the Germans with "The First Noel" and the Germans responded with "O Tannenbaum."

What followed was even more incredible in the midst of a bloody war. Men from both sides put aside their weapons and their animosity, creeping cautiously and quickly together to share food, cigars and drinks and even played a game of soccer together.

What was it that led to unity between foes in the midst of a war, if only for that moment? It was a song about our Savior's birth. But isn't that exactly why the precious Baby was born? Wasn't His mission to bring "peace on earth?"

Whether in times of war or in times of harmony, living in peace is an honorable pursuit. How can we live in peace when we abide in a world of discord? One of the definitions for abide is "to have one's abode; dwell; reside." We reside in this world but we have a choice given us with the birth of a tiny baby over 2,000 years ago. Abide also means to wait in expectation just as Mary waited for the birth of a child who was not of this world but chose to be in this world so we could have ultimate peace.

In Hebrew, the word for "peace" is shalom, meaning "may you be healthy, whole and complete." Peace is more than the absence of conflict. When we recognize peace begins with each of us, we can take steps to reconcile with those from whom we are estranged.

One of my favorite Christmas songs is "Let there be peace on earth."

Let there be peace on earth
And let it begin with me.
Let there be peace on earth
The peace that was meant to be.
With God as our father
Brothers all are we.
Let me walk with my brother
In perfect harmony.

Author Charles Dickens once said, "I have always thought of Christmas time, when it has come round, as a good time; a kind, forgiving, charitable time; the only time I know of, in the long calendar of the year, when men and women seem by one consent to open their shut-up hearts freely, and to think of people below them as if they really were fellow passengers to the grave, and not another race of creatures bound on other journeys."

Are you seeking peace on your journey?

What Are You Giving to Jesus?

"For God so loved the world that he gave His one and only Son that whoever believes in Him shall not perish but have eternal life"—John 3:16 *(NIV)*.

Sometimes Christmas does not fit our expectations of what the perfect holiday should be. We decorate our homes, inside and out. We shop. We wrap gifts. We plan parties or dinners. We attend other holiday events. The days leading up to Christmas pass by faster than the ding of cash registers filling up with cash and credit card receipts. After the wrapping paper is discarded, we can be left with an emptiness that no store-bought gift can fill.

In his book, "Christmas spirit: Memories of Family, Friends and Faith," pastor Joel Osteen writes, "When Christmas doesn't fit your expectations of what the perfect holiday should be, think about how Joseph and Mary probably didn't think the manger was the perfect place for their child to be born. But look at what a perfect Christmas it turned out to be."

A recent devotional was a reminder to seek the real meaning of Christmas. The writer shared a time before Christmas when her husband accidentally broke one of her favorite porcelain teacups while washing dishes. The delicate cup had shattered into so many pieces that glue could not restore it to its original purpose. The tea would have leaked out. Regretfully, she tossed the cup into the trash.

However, on Christmas morning, an unexpected gift of love from her nine-year-old son brought tears to her eyes. Although she had forgotten about the broken teacup, her son had retrieved the pieces from the trash and painstakingly glued them back together. Because the young boy knew how much his mother loved the cup, he had taken time to put it back together. Chipped and scarred with dried glue oozing through some of the cracks, the restored teacup was beautiful in the mother's eyes. Although it would no longer hold tea, it was a reminder to her of the true meaning of Christmas.

The literal meaning of Christmas is "Christ's Mass," referring to a celebration of Christ. However, our current culture doesn't reflect the wonder and awe of that first Christmas over 2,000 years ago. While we search for a joyful Christmas that truly celebrates Christ, so often the holiday season leaves us with very little joy and an elusive emptiness we can't seem to define.

Recently, while having lunch with two friends, our discussion centered on this season, and the needy in our community, especially the children who would not have much at Christmas if it were not for the benevolence of others.

If you want to know the secret to a Christmas holiday filled with love, peace and joy, then look to the manger. The very heart of Christmas came wrapped in swaddling clothes. He was a gift from our Heavenly Father. God loved us so much He sent His only Son that we might be restored to wholeness. It is Jesus' birthday we celebrate on December 25, not ours.

What gift can you give the Christ child? Begin by examining your heart and giving to others who are less fortunate.

Can you do Better?

"Therefore, if anyone is in Christ, the new creation has come: The old has gone, the new is here"– *2 Corinthians 5:17 (NIV)*.

A new year is upon us. My challenge is "Can you do better?"

Hoping to do better and doing better are two different things just as making resolutions and following through are not the same. Whether your resolutions include getting out of debt or losing weight, resolutions don't resolve themselves. The word resolution means "a resolve or determination." Another definition is "the act of resolving or determining upon an action or course of action, method, procedure, etc."

The origin of the word, resolution, has its roots in Latin. From the early fifteenth century, the word means "a breaking into parts." Another meaning is the "process of reducing things into simpler forms." I think that is where we fail to achieve our goals. We can make a resolution to lose weight, even determining the number of pounds we want to lose. We might start out enthused, even signing up for a gym membership.

After several weeks of sweating and groaning, our willpower ebbs and we fall back into old habits. I think it is because we are not specific enough. We set ourselves up for failure when we don't break our goals down into parts. For example, wanting to lose 20 pounds doesn't identify the good habits you need to incorporate into your life each day and which habits are detrimental to your health and need to be addressed, too.

Another popular New Year's Resolution involves finances. It's so easy to get caught up in the secular world of "spend, spend, spend," especially during this time of the year. When those credit card bills come due in January, the holiday hangover can really play havoc with a budget.

While losing weight and getting out of debt are two of the most popular New Year's resolutions, I challenge you to seek God's guidance by asking Him, "Father, where can I do better in the New Year?"

I like this quote by author Gordon B. Hinckley, "Each of us can do a little better than we have been doing. We can be a little more kind. We can be a little more merciful. We can be a little more forgiving. We can put behind us our weaknesses of the past and go forth with new energy and increased resolution to improve the world about us, in our homes, in our places of employment, in our social activities."

One of the most important things we can do in the New Year is to give ourselves a gift that will have far-reaching effects on our health, physically, mentally, emotionally and spiritually.

1 Peter 2:1 tells us to rid ourselves of all malice. Anger, resentment, grudges and a desire for revenge can weigh us down, preventing us from experiencing the joy of the Lord.

Do you need to lose weight for health purposes? Are your finances in a mess? Do you need to be kinder? Maybe you need to forgive someone.

In what area of your life is God calling you to do better?

Do You Have SHD?

"Whether you turn to the right or to the left, your ears will hear a voice behind you, saying, 'This is the way; walk in it'"—Isaiah 30:21 (NIV).

Do you have SHD? What, you mean you've never heard of this disorder? Neither had I until I did some research. SHD is the acronym for Selective Hearing Disorder, meaning we hear what we want to hear. Young children and teenagers are masters of this disorder. So are most adult males.

I recall when my sons were young and I would ask them to pick up their toys. Later, after checking on their progress, I would find they had not followed instructions. When asked why, the reply was usually, "We didn't hear you." Sound familiar?

Other examples of SHD in children include the deer-in-the-headlight look when asked to do chores, eat peas or get ready for bed. Men also suffer from this malady. Have you ever tried to relate an important tidbit of information to a couch potato engrossed in a movie or a football game, only to find out he never heard what you said?

The people of Israel had a hearing problem too. How many warnings did they receive? How many times did God tell them to turn away from their wicked ways, including intermarrying and worshipping idols? The prophet Isaiah was on a mission from God to admonish the people and keep them on the right path.

However, Isaiah wasn't the only prophet who tried to get the people's attention. Jeremiah incessantly warned his people to mend their ways before it was too late. In Jeremiah 5, he says, "Hear this, you foolish and senseless people, who have eyes but do not see, who have ears but do not hear."

Recently, a woman in my Sunday school class shared a story about hearing from God. While Saturday shopping in a nearby town, she was not pleased with the treatment she received at one of the stores where she made purchases. After returning home, she pondered her attitude toward the store personnel and realized she had not been kind with her words or actions. She returned the following Monday, driving more than 20 miles both ways, to apologize. However, the women to whom she needed to ask for forgiveness were not working that day. Upon learning why she wanted to speak to the Saturday employees, the store clerks agreed to relay her message of apology. They were amazed she had returned to admit she had been wrong.

While my friend had not heard God's audible voice, she had listened to that still, small voice convicting her of unacceptable behavior. Because He would not let her forget the wrongness of her bad attitude toward the store clerks, she knew she had to make things right.

Did you know that a synonym for "wrongness" is sin? Are you suffering from SHD?

When was the last time you listened for that still, small voice telling you "this is the way, walk in it?"

Are You Searching for Answers?

"Commit to the Lord whatever you do, and he will establish your plans"
—Proverbs 16:3 (NIV).

Have you ever tried to fill the empty places in your soul with people, possessions or positions? I have. And, I've learned it doesn't work. In my search for answers to life, I ended up on a dead-end road, wondering how in the world I was going to find my way back.

Focused on my job and my accomplishments, I thought it would lead me to the answers. Then, I began to ask myself, "What is the question?" What is it we search for so elusively, spending all of our time, treasures and talent, only to end up with a heart full of emptiness?

At the beginning of a new year, the gyms are filled with people trying to lose weight and get healthy. We make resolutions. I'm going to lose enough to get back into my high school clothes. I want to be able to attend my 20, 30, or 40-year high school reunion looking as good as the day I walked across the stage to get my diploma. Wanting to be healthy is great and doing it for the right reasons leads to success while accepting our aging bodies will never look the same as our 18-year-old self. It is better to focus on our inner life and not so much on the container.

A recent newspaper headline, "Suicide cases rise to 88 in Tulsa," drew my attention. According to the article, the oldest victim was 84 and the youngest was 16. Experts believe that a slow economy and job instability might be to blame, but no one knows for sure.

Growing up, most of us have a plan for our lives. Whether it leads to further education after high school, a fulfilling job, marriage and children, a nice house and a new automobile, we have dreams of a good life. I did. However, our dreams don't always become reality, especially when our focus is on those things that do not fulfill our inner person.

I can relate to those who are so desperate to end their lives. I have been there. However, God had a plan for my life, just as He has a plan for yours. We think life will be perfect when we achieve the "good" things in life. However, when we come to realize, like the author of Ecclesiastes, "that all toil and all achievement spring from one person's envy of another," we can find that one thing that can satisfy forever our thirst for inner peace. If we do not, our life is meaningless, "a chasing after the wind."

Do you feel hollow inside? Is something lacking in your life? Going through the motions of life, even faithfully attending church every Sunday, isn't the answer. The answer is Jesus. He is the only One who can fill that hole inside of us. No possession, person or position can do that. He is the way, the truth and the life.

Have you found the answer?

What Will You Leave Behind?

"Remain in me, as I also remain in you. No branch can bear fruit by itself; it must remain in the vine. Neither can you bear fruit unless you remain in me"--*John 15:4 (NIV)*.

On a recent housecleaning day, I noticed glitter on the floor, on my furniture and even in the bathroom. Puzzled at first, I then realized the sparkly stuff must have come off my granddaughter's t-shirt, the one she had worn the previous day when we celebrated her eighth birthday.

I continued cleaning but could not completely eliminate all traces of the small, shiny objects littering my house. However, as I thought about the previous day and the celebration of a life that God created, I smiled. In the past, the cleaning would have consumed me. After the houseful I had hosted the day before, I would have wanted everything spotless. However, I saw the glittery remains as a reminder of my love for this precious child.

There was another precious child who grew into a man, a man who became our Savior, who reminds us daily that we belong to Him. He didn't stay in the manger. He is not just the baby whose birth we celebrate at Christmas. He is the Living God and He wants a relationship with each one of us.

In a recent sermon, our pastor said, "You belong to God. If your experience with Him ends when you walk out the church door, something is wrong."

I can relate to what my pastor said. Until October 14, 2001, I didn't realize that God wanted a personal relationship with me through His Son. On that warm, sunny Sunday afternoon, I prayed aloud for the first time in my life, asking God to give me direction because I was lost. I was 47-years-old. I had grown up in the church but had walked out the doors, not knowing the truth.

The truth finally set me free, free to be the woman He created me to be, free to grow in His love and grace and free to begin spreading the Good News as all of us should if we are
faithful followers. Pastor Ray explains it this way, "If you've found something satisfying in your heart or soul, you want to share it. It's like one beggar telling another where to find bread."

Jesus is the bread of life. When we grasp with our whole being that He is all we need to satisfy this hunger inside of us, we can't stay quiet. He won't let us. We must choose to make worship a part of our life, to mature in our faith and to leave behind a piece of ourselves wherever we go.

We can set goals and make resolutions. However, if they don't line up with God's plan for our lives, we need to examine the choices we're making. If we want to be kingdom builders, we have to choose now whom we will serve and what our legacy will be.

What will you leave behind?

God's not Through with You Yet

Abraham fell facedown; he laughed and said to himself, "Will a son be born to a man a hundred years old? Will Sarah bear a child at the age of ninety?" –*Genesis 17:17 (NIV).*

Can you imagine the look on the 100-year-old Abraham's face when God promised him a son? Abraham laughed. So did Sarah, who was 90, way past her childbearing years. However, God kept His promise and Isaac was born to the childless couple.

In Genesis 21, we read Sarah's words. "Who would have said to Abraham that Sarah would nurse children? Yet I have borne him a son in his old age."

God wasn't through with Abraham or Sarah yet. While we might not be able to fathom becoming a parent at the ripe old age of 100, God has plans for each one of us, whatever our age.

Adults over age 70 have contributed richly in a variety of ways to our society. At age 74, Emmanuel Kant wrote his finest philosophical works. At age 85, Verdi produced "Ave Maria." Goethe completed "Faust" when he was 80. Tennyson was also 80 when he composed "Crossing the Bar." At age 87, Michelangelo completed what may have been his greatest work.

While you might never have heard of him, George Dawson learned to read at age 98. George had never finished school because he had to quit to help support his family. He was motivated to learn how to read because, he says, "I got tired of writing my name with an X." Four years after learning how to read, the 102-year-old co-authored his autobiography, "Life is Good."

Life is good when we realize our best days are ahead of us even as our bodies are growing frail. Recent conversations with two friends reminded me of this.

One woman, in her mid-80s, lost her husband a year ago. Married for 66 years, he was the love of her life. While I have known some to give up after the death of a spouse, Jackie continues to live her life, even traveling by airplane to visit relatives in another state. She called recently to share some observations she had made about people whom she had met on her travels. Jackie never meets a stranger. As she shared her stories, I knew the strangers she had met would not forget the lessons learned from this wise woman. God is not through with her yet.

Another friend, diagnosed with cancer at 83, is an inspiration to others. After 60+ years of spousal abuse, she had just gone through a divorce the previous year. My friend, however, has shared her story and encouraged younger women who have also suffered abuse. Even after learning about the cancer, she said, "This past year has been the best one of my life."

However, God isn't through with her yet. After overcoming cancer, at age 84, she is still encouraging others who are facing trials.

Did you know God is not through with you either? Life is always an adventure when you trust Him.

The Best Valentine Ever

"I have loved you with an everlasting love; I have drawn you with unfailing kindness"—*Jeremiah 31:3 (NIV)*.

Can you recall your elementary years when you decorated a shoebox with red and pink paper hearts and lace doilies? If you're a male, you might have decorated it with more "manly" colors to take to school on Valentine's Day. Whatever your choice of décor, the box represented something more than a special day to trade the cards, especially made for schoolchildren to exchange. Some of the boxed cards had cartoon themes while others included a heart-shaped sucker. Regardless of the style or theme, the cards and decorated shoeboxes were sometimes a haunting reminder of your popularity (or lack of).

The more popular classmates often received more cards or even nicer cards than those who were not as well liked. If you fit into the latter group, you might not have felt as loved or as valuable as others in your class. It was a day you might have dreaded and were relieved when it was over. It was like being the last one picked for the dodge ball team. You might have avoided meeting people's eyes for fear they could see the pain and the loneliness.

We don't need a reminder of our loneliness when we feel unlovely. Valentine's Day serves as that reminder when often our expectations are unrealistic. We might think we are not worth loving, at least in the way we really want to be loved. However, I have come to realize that when we put that kind of pressure on others, we place a heavy burden on them. Why?

Because no one this side of heaven can love us the way we desire to be loved. Our heavenly Father is the only One who can love us unconditionally—that means warts and all. You see, I was one of those who dreaded Valentine's Day when I was in elementary. Because I was creative, my box might have been one of the best decorated on the outside but the inside was another story.

That applies to each of us. Our outside may be clothed in an array of beautiful garments but our inside is another story. Without His love and peace filling up our empty box, no chocolate candy, glittery cards and flower bouquets will be enough to satisfy the hunger He has placed in each of us to have a relationship with Him.

I sat in my sunroom recently, observing the grays and browns of the winter landscape, when the flash of a cardinal's vivid red feathers reminded me that if we pay attention, we see God's presence everywhere. Our lives can be the same shades of winter. We may feel alone, forgotten or abandoned. We hurt when we think no one cares.

However, the good news is God is crazy about us. He's so crazy in love with us that He sent His only Son to die for you and for me.

Now, that's what I call true love. It's the best Valentine ever.

Does the Shoe Fit?

"However, I consider my life worth nothing to me; my only aim is to finish the race and complete the task the Lord Jesus has given me—the task of testifying to the good news of God's grace" –*Acts 20:24(NIV)*.

My running shoes, showing signs of wear, needed replacing. I hadn't paid attention until my knees started aching. Upon examining the shoes, I realized I had probably put more than 500 miles on this pair. I had quit tracking the number of miles on a pair of shoes when I stopped competing in 5K races over 10 years ago. At the time, I had also belonged to a running club that encouraged us to keep track of our miles to earn prizes. Prizes can be a good motivation sometimes.

When my health insurance company started a walking club, I began logging my daily miles about several months ago. Although I have not totaled the miles yet, my worn shoes and hurting knees reminded me I needed to consider purchasing some new ones, not knees, just shoes. I did, and on the first day of use, my feet and knees thanked me.

I am not athletically gifted. I suffered through sports-related activities during my school years when physical education was required and I was one of the last students chosen for a team. At the time, it was painful, more painful than my aching knees. In my early 40s, I began a walking regimen to get healthy, including the release of stress in my life. One day, my walking partner suggested we enter a 5K race for fun. For me, fun turned into a competition and I began running instead of walking. I became addicted to running. I even won a few trophies and medals in my age division.

I began reading articles about running, trying to learn how to improve my time. Eventually, one small change made all the difference. Instead of focusing on my competition in the race, I began to focus on small goals along the race route. For example, I would focus on a marker along the route. It might be a roadside sign, an electric pole, or some other object in the distance. Once I made it to that point, I would set another small goal. And then another, until the finish line was in view. When that happened, I had enough strength to sprint to the end.

Realizing it wasn't about beating someone else but about doing my personal best, I entered the Tulsa Run, a 15K or 9.32056788 miles to be exact. I set a 90-minute goal. By this time, I just needed to prove to myself that I could finish the race. Although my time was 97 minutes, due to a side stitch that forced me to walk part of the way, I wasn't disappointed.

God expects each of us to do our personal best to finish the race He has called us to run. That's why we have different gifts.

Does your shoe fit? If not, are you trying to wear someone else's shoes?

Hope Arises After the Storm

"Afflicted city, lashed by storms and not comforted, I will rebuild you
with stones of turquoise, your foundations with lapis lazuli"
                                                    –*Isaiah 54:11 (NIV).*

Except for my college years, I have lived most of my life in northeastern
Oklahoma. Prior to my present location, I lived in a community near the
Arkansas and Missouri state lines. It was not unusual for me to drive across
the state lines to shop in larger cities or visit relatives just across the
border. Joplin, Missouri was one of those places. Until recently, it had been
almost two years since my last visit, and that was for my aunt's funeral.

Before a recent February afternoon visit, I had only read stories and seen
photos of the destruction left behind by the EF-5 tornado that ripped
through this southwestern Missouri city on May 22, 2011. I wasn't
prepared for the sight of a flattened landscape dotted with the skeletal
remains of buildings and trees. Although clean-up efforts had begun almost
immediately after the 32-minute storm hit the city, a friend whom I had
come to visit that day revealed the toll that could not be seen, the toll that
still haunts the memories of those who survived one of the deadliest
tornadoes in U.S. history.

As we drove around the city, my emotions were a mixture of disbelief and
shock. Missing landmarks, associated with visits to my Aunt Penny, who
had passed almost a year prior to the day the tornado hit, left me with a
feeling of emptiness. We passed what was left of the Dillon's supermarket
where I took my aunt shopping for groceries. The only concrete evidence
left was the parking lot.

However, houses and businesses are rising from the destruction and more
are being restored in this city of about 50,000. Even with constant
reminders of Mother Nature's fury still evident in buildings not yet torn
down, there is one icon still towering over the debris. The approximately
40 foot weathered iron cross, erected at St. Mary's Catholic Church in the
late 60s, has withstood many previous tornadoes, including the deadly one
that destroyed over 8,000 structures, including businesses, and killed 162
people that Sunday afternoon.

When my friend stopped so I could view the tall iron cross, my hope was
renewed and I knew why the church had chosen to remove all traces of
their destroyed building but leave this symbol as a reminder to all that God

is still present. The church has chosen to rebuild at a different site and the area surrounding the cross will be turned into a park-like memorial where people can come, sit on benches and pray.

This symbol of God's grace will be a reminder to all, both present and future, of our need for Him, not just during our storms but after they have passed. I like this reminder by author Kathy Troccoli, who said, "Jesus Christ is not a security from storms. He is the perfect security in storms."

What are your storms and do you trust Him to see you through them?

Can You Shout Hosanna?

"So they took branches from palm trees and went out to meet him. They shouted, 'Hosanna! Blessed is the one who comes in the name of the Lord!'" —John 12:13(NIRV).

Ash Wednesday was observed last month with the tradition of placing ashes on our foreheads as a sign of repentance to God. Before we began, our pastor reminded us that the ashes were from the burned palm branches waved by the children in the previous year's Palm Sunday service. I was amazed at how the time had flown. Hadn't my grandchildren just joined with other children in the church to march into the sanctuary, waving their palm fronds and shouting, "Hosanna! Hosanna in the highest! Hosanna!"

In the gospel of John, the apostle tells us that Jesus was on His way to Jerusalem when the crowds met Him. As He rode into town on a donkey, the crowds greeted Him with shouts of "Hosanna" and with the waving of palm branches. "Blessed is He who comes in the name of the Lord! Blessed is the King of Israel!"

Zechariah 9:9 foretold this day. "Rejoice greatly, Daughter Zion! Shout, Daughter Jerusalem! See, your king comes to you, righteous and victorious, lowly and riding on a donkey, on a colt, the foal of a donkey."

According to history, the donkey was domesticated in Mesopotamia. Used as a beast of burden and renowned for its strength, the donkey was normally ridden by nonmilitary personnel. However, scripture indicates riding a donkey was not beneath the dignity of Israel's noblemen and kings. 1 Kings 1:32-40 tells us David indicated His choice of Solomon as king by decreeing that the young man should ride on the king's own mule.

Jesus didn't ride into Jerusalem on a war horse but on a lowly beast of burden. While the people, including the disciples, didn't realize the significance of this fulfilled prophecy at the time, the symbolism behind His choice of transportation should not be forgotten today. The Prince of Peace, who came so we all might find peace and rest in His sheltering arms, chose a lowly animal to help announce that He is the Messiah.

How many place hope in the next election, praying that a chosen candidate will lead our government and get us out of this mess? Why do we keep looking for a great military leader to ride in on a stallion and save the day?

How many look to man to help them escape from the problems we have all helped to create? Things are no different today than they were when Jesus rode into Jerusalem that day over 2,000 years ago.

Our Savior didn't come just to liberate us from our worldly adversaries. He wants to free us from all our enemies, from the root of all our problems—sin, evil and death itself. He came to challenge our values and our notions of dominion in every way. So, what are we to do with a Messiah who came in peace, humility, and riding on a lowly donkey?

Can you shout, "Hosanna?"

Are You Fulfilling Your Purpose?

"Create in me a pure heart, O God,
and renew a steadfast spirit within me"—*Psalm 51:10 (NIV).*

"In the beginning, God created the heavens and the earth." Even most people unfamiliar with scripture know the first words in the Bible. The first impression we have of our Heavenly Father when we read this sentence, as well as the rest of Genesis, is of a creator God.

In the beginning, there were no blue skies, no sunlight, no rainbows, no flowers and no trees. There was nothing at all. Then, God spoke. Out of nothing came the sun, the moon, the earth, the mountains, the valleys, the plants and the animals. His loving hands created everything around us. He created it all, including you, including me.

God also created His people to be creators. I had never considered this aspect of creation until I read the following quote by Thomas S. Monson. "God left the world unfinished for man to work his skill upon. He left the electricity in the cloud, the oil in the earth. He left the rivers unbridged, the forests unfelled and the cities unbuilt. God gives to man the challenge of raw materials, not the ease of finished things. He leaves the pictures unpainted and the music unsung and the problems unsolved, that man might know the joys and glories of creation."

Our heavenly Father has a mission for each one of us. Based on the different gifts with which He has blessed us, He challenges us to paint pictures, write songs and stories, discover medical cures, improve our environment, teach others, build churches and hospitals, grow crops and raise livestock. The list is never ending because our Heavenly Father is not through with humanity yet. Not only does He want us to create, He wants us to become the men and women He created us to be.

I compare this process to gardening. Since I love working in my flowerbeds, I like to use this analogy to show the work God wants to do in each of us. First, I have to prepare my beds before planting. I did that recently when I decided to makeover a bed that wasn't doing too well. I removed the old mulch, plucked the weeds, added enriched soil and other nutrients, planted some wildflower seeds, covered them with new mulch and immediately added water to nourish them.

God has to do a makeover on us too. He has to remove any stuff in our lives keeping us from being our best. It often requires plucking, enriching, planting and nourishing. I have discovered that when we are doing what He has called us to do, we find an incredible joy in life. We begin to discover and embrace the person the Lord created each one of us to be. We begin to do those things He created for us to do.

Oswald Chambers once said, "The joy of anything, from a blade of grass upward, is to fulfill its created purpose."

Are you fulfilling your purpose?

How Are You Growing?

"Whenever trouble comes your way, let it be an opportunity for joy. For when your faith is tested, your endurance has a chance to grow"
—*James 1:2-3 (NLT).*

My two-year-old Weeping Willow doubled over as gale force winds struck my neighborhood recently. As I watched the violent storm through my back windows, I prayed that one of my favorite trees could withstand the gusts. Staked out until it was strong enough to survive on its own, the tree's long graceful branches whipped back and forth as if in pain.

The pain of area storms has pummeled our state and the surrounding areas over the past several weeks. Lives have been lost and property destroyed by the onslaught of Mother Nature. Once again, wicked weather has changed many lives. Many will rebuild their lives in the same area. Others will decide to move on.

Storms and trials in our personal lives can produce growth if we allow it. Weathering our storms teaches us that God is faithful and will provide the strength to stand firm. When I read that the willow tree, flexible and unlike other trees, can bend without breaking, I was touched by the following truth. The willow tree has the ability to adjust and adapt to life rather than fight it. The willow tree grows very large, often developing from a solitary branch that has fallen into a watery area. This graceful tree not only grows in less than optimal conditions, it thrives. If we relate the willow's growing ability and flexibility to humanity, it becomes a symbol for us to keep growing and reaching, regardless of where God plants us and what life's storms bring.

Author Marilyn Bateman once said, "So often the things that teach us the most and give us the greatest insights into God's ways happen while we are struggling. If we turn to God for strength, feelings and sure knowledge pour into our thinking through the light that quickens our understanding."

Understanding this life-changing truth makes a difference. Jesus did not come to banish the storms in our lives. He came to fill us with His presence in the midst of them. Our peace and confidence must be deeply rooted in God. If we are to weather life's trials and raging storms, we must choose the joy that comes from knowing His ways are higher than our ways. We can fight the storms or we can celebrate them, even when they don't make sense.

In John 16:33, Jesus says, "I have told you these things, so that in me you may have peace. In this world, you will have trouble. But take heart! I have overcome the world."

With our human logic, we want to define life on our terms. Faith, however, is a matter of blind obedience. If we choose to trust and obey Him, He gives us the strength to withstand any storm in our lives.

Is there a storm raging in your life today? Let your Heavenly Father use it to help you grow stronger roots in Him and count it all as joy.

Are You Sharing Dessert?

"Here is a boy with five small barley loaves and two small fish, but how far will they go among so many?"—*John 6:9 (NIV).*

Baked fudge with whipped cream, coconut cream pie, strawberry cheesecake, molten chocolate cake, peach cobbler. I watched as two women at a local restaurant perused the menu, trying to decide which dessert they would choose. They finally agreed on the coconut cream pie, which they shared.

Sharing a dessert after a restaurant meal is a wise idea, considering the portions now offered. I'm not complaining because I usually ask for a doggie bag, not to take the leftovers home to my dog, but to have a second meal at home. This accomplishes two things. First, I don't have to cook. Second, I don't have to cook again because I am eating my restaurant leftovers.

Do you remember the story of leftovers in the Bible? Known as the miracle of the five loaves and two fishes, the story appears in all four gospels. Apart from the resurrection story, it is the only miracle appearing in Matthew, Mark, Luke and John. John is the only gospel to mention a boy who had brought his lunch of fish and bread, which he willingly shared with the others.

According to scripture, it was Passover time in Israel, which meant a holiday. However, the people, including Jesus, were saddened by the news of the beheading of John the Baptist as ordered by King Herod. A grieving Jesus wanted to get away by himself to pray. To escape the massive crowds who were following Him, Jesus boarded a boat to sail across the Sea of Galilee where He could find solitude.

However, the crowds followed along the shoreline, keeping an eye on His boat. When Jesus landed, He was greeted by a multitude of 5,000, clamoring to hear His teachings. Was Jesus angry or irritated? No, He looked on the crowd with compassion and as the daylight waned, one of the disciples said, "Lord, the hour is late and the people don't have any food and we are a long way from any villages. Maybe you should send them home now."

Jesus, however, chose to use a little boy's five loaves of bread and two fish to perform a miracle. After inviting everyone to sit on the grass, Jesus took the bread, looked up into heaven, gave thanks, broke it and then gave it to His disciples to distribute to the crowds. All ate and were satisfied. And guess what, there were even leftovers. Scripture tells us that twelve baskets of bread remained after everyone had eaten their fill.

The little boy surrendered his meager gifts to Christ. God, in His abundant generosity, used them to bless the multitudes. We, too, are called to a life of generous giving. However, we shouldn't just give our leftovers, we should share the best we have to offer. When we do that, you can bet God will use us, and our gifts, for His purposes.

Are you sharing your dessert?

You Have a Choice

"The heavens tell about the glory of God.
The skies show that His hands created them" *–Psalm 19:1 (NIRV).*

Storm clouds forecast a gloomy day when I went out to retrieve my morning paper. With no sun in sight, a recent Monday reminded me of a 1971 song called "Rainy Days and Mondays."

Part of the lyrics seems to describe many people's lives. "Hangin' around, nothing to do but frown; rainy days and Mondays always get me down." While it's true that too many overcast days can affect our moods, we have the ability to choose our thoughts and attitudes. Pastor Chuck Swindoll says, "The remarkable thing is we have a choice everyday regarding the attitude we will embrace for that day."

I could have chosen to let the overcast skies define my outlook that day. However, I chose to take my dog for an early morning walk. The cool breeze was a welcome respite from the unseasonably warm and humid temperatures. I said, "Thank you, Lord," as the light wind blew across my face.

As we walked through our neighborhood, I noticed the array of spring flowers, each species distinguished by different colors, shapes and sizes. What an awesome God we serve! He could have created all flowers the same. How boring? Instead, our creative, loving Father wanted us to experience a kaleidoscope of ever changing patterns of color and shapes to delight our eyes and bring peace to our weary souls.

During the early day journey through our community, we encountered a multitude of wild rabbits enjoying the same cooler weather as well as the neighbors' flowers. While I enjoyed watching their antics, my dog strained at his leash, begging me to let him give chase.

Why do humans spend their lives chasing riches and fame when God, in all His glory, has already given us so much beauty and pleasure in His creation? In Ecclesiastes, wise King Solomon says, "And I saw that all toil and all achievement spring from one person's envy of another. This too is meaningless, a chasing after the wind."

We will never catch the wind. We can't even see it. We can, however, feel it and see its effects on nature. We can't see God either. However, we can see His presence in all creation, and if we take the time, we can experience His presence in the quietness of an early morning. Hebrews 3:1 says, "Therefore, holy brothers and sisters, who share in the heavenly calling, fix your thoughts on Jesus, whom we acknowledge as our apostle and high priest." When we seek Jesus each morning, He changes our attitude about life. It requires, however, that we keep our focus on Him.

Pastor Joel Osteen says, "Choosing to be positive and having a grateful attitude is going to determine how you're going to live your life." We can spend our lives yearning for what others have or we can enjoy what God has already provided.

How will you choose to live? Will it be in gratitude for His creation? If so, what are you thankful for today?

What Does Prayer Mean to You?

"This, then, is how you should pray:
"'Our Father in heaven,
hallowed be your name,
your kingdom come,
your will be done,
on earth as it is in heaven."
—*Matthew 6:8-10 (NIV)*.

When they asked how, Jesus taught his disciples to pray. The Lord's Prayer, found in Matthew 6:8-14, reveals our Savior's heart. What does prayer mean to you? Do you think it's a mysterious practice reserved for the religiously devout?

Prayer is simply a conversation with your Abba Father. Minister and author, Josh McDowell, has this to say about prayer: "Prayer is talking with God. God knows your heart and is not so concerned with your words as He is with the attitude of your heart."

For some, even Christians, prayer has become an afterthought, done only while sitting in a church pew, at the dinner table or beside a child's bed before sleep. Sometimes, prayer is offered as a wish of one's heartfelt desire with expectations of God answering like a genie inside a magic lamp.

If you're seeking an intimate, powerful transformation in your relationship with God, then your prayer life must be more than asking for things. Praying is not just setting aside a special time to spend with Him; it is an ongoing conversation with Him throughout your busy day. While you are at work, eating, conversing with others, waiting for appointments or on the run from one place to another, you can be in prayer. Thank Him continually for the blessings in your life, even the difficult times. They help you to grow closer to Him.

However, starting the day with Him is vital for your spiritual growth. When I sit down with my Bible and prayer journal each morning, I am consciously choosing to give Him the first part of my day. It's the same principle as tithing. Giving Him the first fruits of your day reveals your priorities.

Prayer is a time to remind yourself that everything you are, and everything you have, comes through the power, grace and mercy of the one true God. Communion through prayer allows a deeper connection between His Word, His Holy Spirit and yourself, allowing seeds of faith to be firmly planted within your being.

How does a conversation with God begin? Get quiet. Seek a special place where you can open your mind, soul and spirit to what He has to say to you, both in that still, small voice, and within the pages of your Bible. Seeking Him requires you to listen more than you speak. Ask Him to reveal Himself to you. Remember what Josh McDowell said, "God knows your heart and is not so concerned with your words as He is with the attitude of your heart."

It's about your heart connection to the One who loves you more than life itself. We must remember that it's not about you and it's not about me. It's about God and His will.

Then, you will realize that your prayers will touch the heart of the One for whom nothing is impossible.

Do You Trust God with Your Time?

"So teach us to number our days that we may get a heart of wisdom"–
Psalm 90:12 (ESV).

Have you ever wished for more hours in your day? I have. In the past, with to-do-list and calendar in hand, I thought I was in control of the universe. God had to teach me otherwise. While having a calendar and to-do-list is important to manage our time wisely, we must examine what is penned on each one in light of eternal value.

In a recent essay, author Mary Southerland says, "Time management is a dreaded and often ignored spiritual discipline for many of us. We have either forgotten or failed to realize the truth that our minutes, hours and days are precious commodities—gifts from God that can be unwrapped only once. Time is wasted unless it is invested in goals and priorities that are rooted in God's plan."

Many of us equate a busy life as a productive one. We try to justify our busy life by pointing out our list of "good things." However, my to-do-list, filled with what I thought were "good things" was not God's list. Inked on each line was not God's plan for my life but my own selfish desire to accomplish more—and for all the wrong reasons.

In his book, "First Thing Every Morning," Lewis Timberlake offers six terrific truths about time. First, "nobody can manage time." However, you can manage those things that take up your time. Second, says Timberlake, "time is expensive." In fact, "80 percent of our day is spent on those things or those people that only bring us two percent of our results." Third, he points out "time is perishable. It cannot be saved for later use."

According to Timberlake's fourth truth, "Time is measurable. Everybody has the same amount of time...pauper or king. It is not how much time you have; it is how much you use." His fifth truth is similar. "Time is irreplaceable. We never make back time once it is gone."

Finally, he says, "Time is a priority. You have enough time for anything in the world, so long as it ranks high enough among your priorities."

If we don't set priorities, others will do it for us. When I allowed others, along with my list of to-do's to control my life, there was no time for God.

While we have different priorities during different seasons of our lives, one priority should remain steadfast. In Matthew 6:33, Jesus says, "But put God's kingdom first. Do what he wants you to do. Then all of those things will also be given to you."

Once I put God at the top of my list, the rest of life fell into place. By giving Him the first fruits of my day, He guides my steps and my time becomes focused on His will for my life. Spending early morning time in prayer, Bible reading and journaling opens my eyes and heart to His timing.

Do you trust God with your time?

When Your Pot Overflows

"And my God will meet all your needs according to the riches
of his glory in Christ Jesus"– *Philippians 4:19 (NIV)*

While I was engrossed in a writing project, an unattended pot of soup
overflowed, leaving a mess on my stovetop. The soup was a concoction of
just about everything I could find in my pantry and freezer. Preparing it for
an ill neighbor, I wanted to avoid going to the grocery store if I had
ingredients on hand.

In my pantry, I located cans of beef stock. My freezer was full of frozen
veggies. I added green beans, corn, carrots, cauliflower, broccoli, spinach,
zucchini and yellow squash, along with some mini meatballs I had
previously frozen. After browsing through my spice rack, which I had
recently cleaned to toss outdated cans and bottles, I added oregano leaves
and some parsley flakes. After adding a tad of fresh garlic, I put the lid on
the pot. In my hurry to focus on my writing, I set the temperature too high.

As my fingers flew across the keyboard, I completely forgot about my
neighbor's meal. Until I heard the sizzle of liquid meeting the electric coils
of my stove, I was completely oblivious to my surroundings. I tend to do
that when the writing muse consumes me.

Our lives can be like that. Our wants can consume us so we forget to count
our blessings. A recent conversation with someone reminded me of this.
We were discussing repairs that needed to be made to his pickup truck. To
save money, he was fixing the vehicle himself. However, purchasing the
necessary parts had drained funds set back for something he had wanted.
When he realized he would have to start saving again, he was frustrated.

I reminded him that God had provided the funds because He knew they
would be needed for truck repairs, which were a necessity. I also shared
with this young man a recent habit I had begun. After reading an article
about a man who had saved every five-dollar bill for three years, I began
doing the same. In that three-year time span, he had accumulated $12,000.

While I don't know what this man did with his money, I am sure that when
he set out on his journey, he didn't realize how much he would have in
three years. However, it is not about how much we have in the material
world, but how much of God we have in our lives.

In Psalm 73:26, the writer says, "My flesh and my heart may fail, but God
is the strength of my heart and my portion forever."

When we are feeling weak and helpless, the Lord provides a sufficient portion of strength. His grace sustains us through times of anxiety, discouragement, frustration and weariness. We can spin our wheels searching for joy and satisfaction in earthly things while God patiently waits for us to realize that we really need more of Him.

Next time your pot overflows say, "Thank you, Lord, for your provision."

When You Put Things in Perspective

"I have told you these things, so that in me you may have peace. In this world you will have trouble. But take heart! I have overcome the world"
—*John 16:33 (NIV)*.

One recent morning, I noticed my Hollyhocks, which had achieved a height of more than eight feet, were lying on the ground. Looking around, I discovered the source of my downed flowers when I saw rainwater flowing through the wet weather creek in the field behind my house. I had slept so soundly I had not heard the storm passing through during the night.

Retrieving my newspaper, I noticed more evidence of the storm. Some of my flowerbeds had been relieved of their mulch by the heavy rains. At first, I was exasperated because mulch is not cheap, especially when you have as many flowerbeds as I do. Glancing down the street, I noticed debris scattered across two of my neighbors' yards. I suspected their homes had been flooded because one had experienced flooding problems before. This time, both houses had damage.

I knocked on their doors to offer my help. Giving my friend, Ella, a hug, I asked what I could do. She replied, "Pray for us." Ella put things in perspective when she said, "This is nothing compared to losing my son." Ella lost an adult son several years ago in a kayaking accident. She said, "You can replace things but you can't replace a loved one."

Ella is so right. My first reaction to the missing mulch was trivial. How easy it is to get caught up in our troubles. Other words for perspective are view or outlook. If we viewed our temporary troubles in light of God's kingdom, they seem minor.

Jesus said, "In this world you will have trouble." We can take comfort from His words because He has overcome the world. If we allow Him to, He will bring peace when life floods us with uncertainty.

A survivor of the Holocaust, Corrie Ten Boom, said, "Often I have heard people say, 'How good God is! We prayed that it would not rain for our church picnic, and look at the lovely weather!' Yes, God is good when He sends good weather. But God was also good when He allowed my sister, Betsie, to starve to death before my eyes in a German concentration camp. I remember one occasion when I was very discouraged there. Everything around us was dark, and there was darkness in my heart. I remember telling Betsie that I thought God had forgotten us. 'No, Corrie,' said Betsie, 'He has not forgotten us. Remember His Word: 'For as the heavens are high above the earth, so great is His steadfast love toward those who fear Him.' Corrie concludes, 'There is an ocean of God's love available—there is plenty for everyone. May God grant you never to doubt that victorious love—whatever the circumstances.'"

What are your circumstances today? Do you trust God to help you put things in perspective?

Have You Talked to God Lately?

"The Lord is near to all who call on him,
to all who call on him in truth"—Psalm 145:18 (NIV).

What would you do if one of your teenagers sent a text message from her bedroom one morning, asking you to fix cinnamon rolls for breakfast? This was the recent scenario in an area newspaper article titled, "Is texting ruining the art of conversation?"

Mom yelled upstairs, telling her daughter, "If you want to talk to me, come downstairs and see me." The teenager later admitted that she had been lazy that morning. According to the article, this is not a fictional account but an increasingly typical way of communication, especially among younger people.

Statistics released by the Pew Internet & American Life Project recently revealed that many people with cell phones today prefer texting to a phone call. Although it's not always the younger generation, statistics do indicate that the younger you are, the more likely you are to prefer this method of communication. While some argue it's no big deal, the different method of communication between the talkers and the texters can lead to an even bigger gap in relationships. While there's nothing wrong in casual texting conversations, some communications experts believe the problem lies in the decline of deeper, more meaningful conversations.

When was the last time you had a meaningful conversation with God? I don't mean just asking for something, but a one-on-one talk with your Heavenly Father. TV evangelist, Joyce Meyer, says, "Too often we spend all of our time seeking God for answers to our problems when what we should be doing is just seeking God."

When was the last time you sought His presence and not a handout? "Prayer isn't some kind of requirement for Believers," says author Christa Kinda. "It is a privilege."

In some countries, Believers live in fear for their lives. If they are caught worshipping God, it can mean death. In America, it's a freedom to be able to worship and pray. Yet, how often do we take for granted that freedom?

We have an even greater freedom found in our Savior, Jesus Christ. In John 8, Jesus says, "If you abide in my word, you are truly my disciples, and you will know the truth, and the truth will set you free."

The truth is God wants you to call on Him. He wants a personal relationship with each one of His children, not just a superficial one based on "give me, give me, give me," like a short text message.

Your Heavenly Father wants you to know Him and understand His plans and purposes for your life. If you wrestle with trying to understand where your life is headed and live a life of fear, you are doomed to drift aimlessly through life if you don't consult the One who made you.

Scripture tells us to "Be still, and know that I am God." In a world of 24/7 distractions, we need to remember to be still if we want to have a conversation with Him.

Have you talked to your Heavenly Father lately?

Do You Know Where you are Going?

"Many are the plans in a person's heart,
but it is the LORD's purpose that prevails"—Proverbs 19:21 (NIV).

Two directionally-challenged women recently returned from a 2,000-mile journey to the east coast. We left northeastern Oklahoma equipped with an atlas, MapQuest driving directions and my new GPS, which I dubbed "Shirley." Don't ask me why I chose that name, it just popped in my head while we were on our road trip to Atlanta, Georgia.

"Shirley" did not come with extensive written operating instructions. Although simpler is better in some cases, this woman, meaning me, is not tech-savvy. I even went to the manufacturer's website before our June 15 departure to get detailed directions for "her" use. I also made three trips to the store where I purchased the instrument prior to "D" day for assistance with "Shirley." I know the clerks were probably laughing at a woman who prefers a Rand-McNally map in her hands to a female voice telling her to go right, go left or to make a u-turn when she doesn't listen.

I'm certain that God is disappointed, and sometimes entertained, by our human tendency to ignore His voice. I can just hear Him saying, "Why don't you listen, my child? Things would be so much easier if you would just pay attention to my directions."

I'm also certain that God allows u-turns when we get off the path He has planned for us. Even when we ignore that still, small voice telling us to go right and then turn left, He gently corrects us, leading us back on the right path if we are open. Did you know that God speaks to you if you will only listen?

How do we listen? First, we must come to God and surrender our will. For me, a recovering control freak, the process is still sometimes a struggle. However, I have discovered that by taking it one day at a time, and sometimes one hour at a time, it's easier to lean on Him for direction. I have also learned that surrendering control to Him frees me to become the woman He wants me to be. Surrender has a negative connotation in man's vocabulary. Not so in God's dictionary. God's definition equates surrender with freedom.

It takes courage to walk in freedom. One of the antonyms, or the opposite of the word freedom, is captivity. While we may not be locked behind bars, we can still be a prisoner of our own poor choices.

Musician David Stephens once said, "Freedom is the fragrance of grace." God's grace frees us from the invisible chains holding us from His best. When we choose to follow His path, our lives are transformed into something better, even in the things we have imagined, expected, or hoped for.

Proverbs 3:5-6 says, "Trust in the Lord with all your heart and lean not on your own understanding; in all your ways acknowledge Him, and He will make your paths straight."

Following God's purpose for our life is rewarding. Do you know where you are going?

Other Books by Carol

A Matter of Faith
ISBN-10: 0937660450 124 pages $12.95
Available from Amazon.com and other retailers

In this collection of her faith-based columns, Carol Round uses everyday experiences to inspire her readers to seek a deeper relationship with the Lord. Her weekly faith-based column is currently available in 12 Oklahoma newspapers and one on-line publication, http://www.assistnews.net/.

"Carol's comforting writing style is soothing and her sage advice is enlightening. Each selection draws the reader's attention to things that are really important. She frequently ends her column with an appropriate action (Whom do you need to forgive?) or challenge (Make a difference.) for the reader."—*Rebecca Johnson, Amazon Top 10 Book Reviewer*

Faith Matters
ISBN-10: 0937660833 124 pages $12.95
Available from Amazon.com and other retailers

Carol Round's weekly faith-based column, "A Matter of Faith," has inspired over 200,000 readers since it first debuted in November 2005. In this second collection of her columns, she uses everyday experiences to encourage her readers to seek a deeper relationship with the Lord.

"Ms. Round has the nice ability to meld Biblical inspiration with everyday humility to see new wonders of living through our Lord, Jesus Christ." – *Professor Donald Mitchell, Amazon.com Top Reviewer*

Journaling with Jesus: How to Draw Closer to God
ISBN-10: 1449736610 84 pages $9.95
Available from Amazon.com and other retailers

"*Journaling with Jesus* is a creative call to an authentic, intimate relationship with Christ through the art of prayer-journaling. Author Carol Round openly shares her own intimate journaling journey, initially borne of pain, and now bathed in promise--the hope of healing in Jesus. Let her sensitively guide you along your own prayer path through balanced Scriptural support, stories from the lives of women transformed through the power of journaling, encouraging explanations about the benefits of journaling, and timely tips about how to start. Allow *Journaling with Jesus* to take you deep into the heart of God, by showing you practically and inspirationally how to bare the depths of your own heart on the blank page. As you fill your journal with words of honesty, God will fill your heart with the wonder of His love."—*Lynn D. Morrissey, author of "Love Letters to God: Deeper Intimacy through Written Prayer"*

The 40 Day Challenge: A companion workbook to Journaling with Jesus: How to Draw Closer to God
ISBN-10: 0615691714   60 pages $12.95
Available from Amazon.com and other retailers

Are you as close to God as you would like to be? *The 40 Day Challenge* is a companion workbook to *Journaling with Jesus: How to Draw Closer to God*, which challenges readers to try prayer journaling for 40 days. The workbook, as the title says, is a 40-day challenge with each day including a scripture, thoughts about that day's challenge, a short prayer to our Abba Father, blank lines to write your own love letter to God and a follow-up "faith step" to take on your journey to know Him better.

"Carol Round discovered prayer journaling, as she focused on the pain and confusion of an empty nest and a recent divorce. As the mornings passed, she found healing, growth, and potential in seeking deeper intimacy with God. Based on her experiences, Round encourages and challenges her readers to record their spiritual journey in a daily prayer journal over a forty-day period. The author's style and manner invite and let the reader look over the writer's shoulder with impunity and promise, with commitment and covenant, with action and accountability."
—*Jorja Davis, Amazon reviewer*

About the Author

If someone were to ask me why I write, I would have to reply, "Why not?" It is part of who I am. As a child, my love of a good story often got me into trouble at school. I would hide my library book, usually a mystery, behind the pages of a bulky school text. That is probably the reason my grades suffered in other areas, especially math.

At night, my mother would often find me hiding under the bed sheets reading. This was after she had told me more than once to turn out the lights and go to sleep. I focused on the page with the help of a flashlight I had pilfered from Dad. As with most avid readers, I love the written word. I had dreams of being a famous writer one day, cut off from civilization, living life like Thoreau. I had no trouble, even as a child, imagining what it would be like to live on Walden Pond.

Because of my fascination with nature, my first attempts at writing were about God's divine creation. I wrote rhyming poems to express my love for everything outdoors: the spring flowers, the fall colors, dancing snowflakes and summer showers. I cringe now at my early endeavors because although I very seldom write poetry today, I prefer free verse.

For me, writing has become more than just playing with words. During times of trouble in my life, the written word has served as a catharsis. Keeping a journal, writing letters to God or making a list of goals has helped me to regroup, refocus and redefine my life.

After taking a six-week fiction-writing course at a community college, I completed ten chapters of a romantic suspense novel. Even though the writing instructor said I had a talent for that genre, I could never finish the book. I was going through a rough time in my life—separation and eventually a divorce. Only after this painful experience did I come to realize what was missing in my life. I grew up in the church. I believed in God. I knew of Him, but I didn't know Him.

As my relationship with the Lord has grown, so has my writing. Knowing Him has opened my heart, my eyes and my ears to a deeper understanding of life. With a wisdom born from failure and forgiveness, I have committed my writing to His glory.

At my core, I am a woman seeking more of Him and His will for my life. I hope one day to hear those wonderful words, ***"Well done, my good and faithful servant."***

To My Readers

I would love to hear your feedback. You may contact me via email at *carolaround@yahoo.com*. You can also receive my weekly column by email. Just drop me a note. If you like this book, would you please go to Amazon.com, write a review, and share it with your friends? Also, please feel free to connect with me at:

- Blog:
  www.carolaround.com

- Book website:
  http://www.journalingwithjesus.com

- Facebook page:
  http://www.facebook.com/carolaround
  (Please be sure and "friend" me.)

- Facebook fan page:
  http://www.facebook.com/JournalingwithJesus
  (Please be sure and "like" my page.)

- My other Facebook fan page:
  http://www.facebook.com/pages/A-Matter-of-Faith/132121790200971
  (Please be sure and "like" my page.)

- Twitter:
  http://twitter.com/carolaround

- Utube:
  http://www.youtube.com/watch?v=0SJDd1L5VFs:
  "Journaling with Jesus: How to Draw Closer to God" book trailer
  (Please click "like" and share it with your friends.)

- My Amazon.com author page:
  http://www.amazon.com/Carol-Round/e/B0083ZEAWI/ref=sr_ntt_srch_lnk_1?qid=1342565567&sr=1-1
  (Please be sure and "like" my page.)

What others
are saying about

A Matter of Faith & Faith Matters

"I started reading *Faith Matters* and I could not put it down. If there is a term called 'spot on' this book was it. There is so much to take away and learn from this beautifully written book. It definitely reveals that God wants to be a constant part of our everyday life and if we pay attention, we will realize that He really is. This is a great source for anyone who is looking for his or her best life yet."
—*Val Newton-Bowles, Amazon reviewer*

"I love Carol Round's warm cheerful writing style that draws you into her stories. In *Faith Matters,* she shares her well-earned wisdom. I especially enjoyed reading the list of gifts that don't cost a penny. It reminds me to be a better listener or to write a note to a friend. You will be blessed by reading this beautiful book, which will encourage you to think more deeply about life and how fortunate you really are to be alive."
— *Rebecca Johnson, Amazon Top 10 Book Reviewer*

"As I read *Faith Matters,* I realized how much we have in common. Or maybe it's not just me, but she has a way of resonating with women in general. She writes with a tone that is warm and encouraging. This is an easy-to-read book that I highly recommend!"
—*Kimberly Payne, Amazon reviewer*

"*A Matter of Faith* is filled with everyday wisdom without preachiness. Each essay is motivating, enjoyable, and written in a warm conversational tone." —*Geni J. White, Amazon reviewer*

"Down-to-earth and uplifting describe the writing style of author Carol Round in her book *A Matter of Faith.* Carol has the ability to weave Biblical truths, personal experience and thought-provoking questions into a format more akin to a comfortable conversation with a friend than a formal spiritual treatise. Each column reminded me that relationship with GOD doesn't have to be a formal exercise, but rather a daily act of growing closer as we live life with HIM. Thank you, Carol."
—*Clayton Bates, Amazon reviewer*

What others
are saying about

Journaling with Jesus: How to Draw Closer to God
and *The 40-Day Challenge*

"Journaling is an age-old practice of examining one's life. It is a tremendous tool to track and measure learning, growth, and change. It can make a dramatic difference, especially when Jesus is invited into the process. That is what this book is all about. **I highly recommend** you get Carol's book and allow her journaling process to assist, enhance, and inspire yours."

—Nancy Slocum, Amazon review

"Allow ***Journaling with Jesus*** to take you deep into the heart of God, by showing you practically and inspirationally how to bare the depths of your own heart on the blank page. As you fill your journal with words of honesty, God will fill your heart with the wonder of His love."

—Lynn D. Morrissey, author
"Love Letters to God: Deeper Intimacy through Written Prayer"

"Blessed to know that this little but very deep and **wonderful book points straight to God and His Words** as our basis to start with daily prayer journaling and to learn to understand them, which helps us understand God and His ways."

—Karen Lyons, LyonsLady blog

"Do you desire to have a more intimate relationship with the Lord? Are you unsure about how to achieve it? Carol Round's book will inspire, encourage, and—perhaps perhaps best of all—give you practical guidance on how to develop a closer walk and open up the lines of communication between you and God through journaling. Whether or not/however you journal, **this book will help you 'amp up' your prayer life**. Clearly, succinctly, and honestly written, you will find it helpful on a number of levels."

—Paula Smith, Amazon review

5224607R00137

Made in the USA
San Bernardino, CA
30 October 2013